ALASKA'S MOUNTAIN RANGES

by George Wuerthner

American Geographic Publishing

William A. Cordingley, Chairman
Rick Graetz, Publisher
Mark Thompson, Director of Publications
Barbara Fifer, Production Manager

Library of Congress Cataloging-in-Publication Data

Wuerthner, George.
    Alaska's mountain ranges.

    1. Mountains--Alaska.   I. Title.
GB525.5.A4W84 1988   917.98'02   88-24263
ISBN 0-938314-58-0 (pbk.)

ISBN 0-938314-58-0
© 1988 American Geographic Publishing,
Box 5630, Helena, MT 59604.
(406) 443-2842

Text © 1988 George Wuerthner.
Design by Linda Collins.
Printed in Hong Kong.

This book is dedicated to all m
friends who joined me on one
Alaskan wilderness adventure c
another, in particula, Al Sanders
Anchorage, who for many years
my most constant traveling partr
Al's sense of humor and easy-goi
manner made these mountain
explorations all the more enjoyal

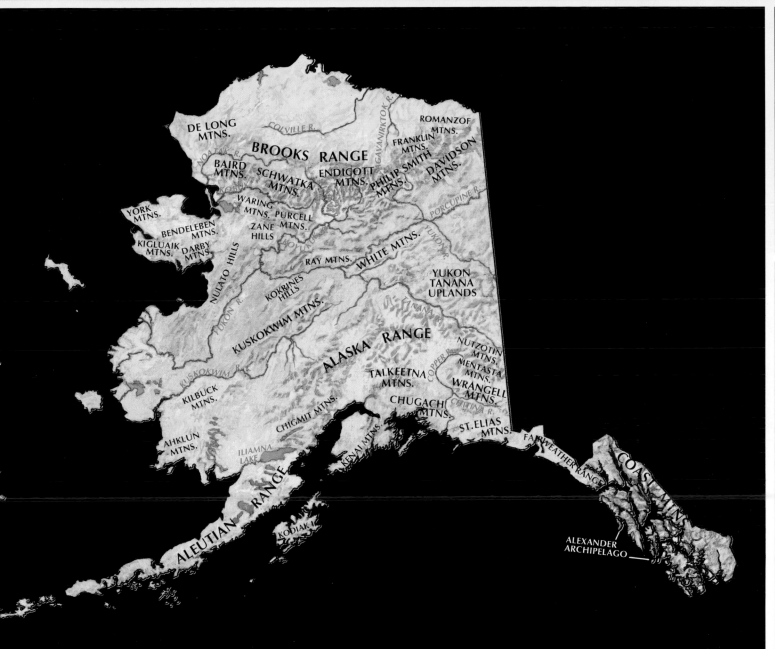

DE LONG MTNS.

COLVILLE R.

ROMANZOF MTNS.

BROOKS RANGE

FRANKLIN MTNS.

NOATAK R.

BAIRD MTNS.

SCHWATKA MTNS.

ENDICOTT MTNS.

PHILIP SMITH MTNS.

DAVIDSON MTNS.

GAVANIRKTOK R.

KOBUK R.

PORCUPINE R.

YORK MTNS.

WARING MTNS.

PURCELL MTNS.

BENDELEBEN MTNS.

ZANE HILLS

KOYUKUK R.

KIGLUAIK MTNS.

DARBY MTNS.

RAY MTNS.

WHITE MTNS.

YUKON R.

NULATO HILLS

KOKRINES HILLS

YUKON TANANA UPLANDS

YUKON R.

KUSKOKWIM MTNS.

ALASKA RANGE

NUTZOTIN MTNS.

KUSKOKWIM R.

TALKEETNA MTNS.

COPPER R.

MENTASTA MTNS.

KILBUCK MTNS.

CHUGACH MTNS.

WRANGELL MTNS.

CHITINA R.

CHIGMIT MTNS.

ST. ELIAS MTNS.

AHKLUN MTNS.

ILIAMNA LAKE

KENAI MTNS.

FAIRWEATHER RANGE

COAST MTNS.

ALEUTIAN RANGE

KODIAK I.

ALEXANDER ARCHIPELAGO

Front cover: Tundra pond and Mt. McKinley, Denali National Park. LARRY ULRICH
Back cover: Toe of Exit Glacier near Seward. BRUCE SELYEM
Title page: Shoulder of Fan Mountain near headwaters of the Anktuvuk River, Brooks Range. GEORGE WUERTHNER
Facing page, top: Beached icebergs at Muir Inlet, Glacier Bay National Park. GEORGE WUERTHNER
Bottom: Bluebells frame miner's shack at Nabesna in the Wrangell Mountains. GEORGE WUERTHNER
Above: Iceberg by Wellesley Glacier, College Fiord, Chugach Mountains. GEORGE WUERTHNER

3

ABOUT THE AUTHOR

The author unloading his kayak at Reid Inlet, Glacier Bay National Park. GEORGE WUERTHNER PHOTO

George Wuerthner has traveled widely throughout Alaska and has visited all but one of the state's national parks, preserves and monuments. He has been employed in Alaska by the BLM as a surveyor, as well as a river ranger on the Fortymile Wild and Scenic River. He also worked as a ranger in the Gates of the Arctic National Park. Outside Alaska, Wuerthner has been employed as a botanist, university instructor, guide and high school teacher.

Between jobs, Wuerthner has taken many Alaskan wilderness journeys—some up to four months in duration and covering various portions of the state by kayak, canoe and ski.

He is the author of three other books including *Oregon Mountain Ranges, Idaho Mountain Ranges, The Adirondacks: Forever Wild,* and co-author with Mollie Matteson of *Vermont: Portrait of the Land and Its People.* His photography and writings have appeared in numerous national publications.

When not traveling he makes his home in Livingston, Montana just north of Yellowstone National Park.

ACKNOWLEDGMENTS

Despite my extensive travels in Alaska, I had to rely upon many different sources for additional information about the state's history, geology, wildlife and other topics. I am indebted to Mountain Press Publishing of Missoula, Montana who allowed me to review portions of their *Roadside Geology of Alaska* prior to publication. I also found many of the books published by Alaska Northwest Publishing to be useful references, along with federal and state public documents. To all these other authors I owe a debt of gratitude.

CONTENTS

Left: *Peaks of the Chugach Mountains rise to 10,000′ above the waters of Harriman Fiord.* GEORGE WUERTHNER
Facing page, top: *Birch leaves line a tributary of the Fortymile River.* GEORGE WUERTHNER
Bottom: *Bull caribou.* PAT POWELL

INTODUCTION

One of the most notable features of Alaska is its abundance of mountains and hills. The only expansive stretches of flat terrain are the North Slope and Yukon-Kuskokwim deltas, with smaller amounts of relatively level ground in the Kobuk-Selawik delta, Susitna River, Yukon Flats, Minto Flats and Bristol Bay areas. Yet, even these areas are bounded by mountains.

Most of these highlands fall into three broad mountain belts: the 600-mile-long Brooks Range, which stretches across the northern end of the state, and the equally long Alaska Range arcing across the southern portion of the state north of Anchorage. The third major mountain arc follows the coast beginning in Southeast Alaska and stretching along the Gulf of Alaska to the Alaskan Peninsula. It includes the St. Elias Range, Chugach Mountains, Kenai Mountains and the mountains of Kodiak Island.

Of the 20 highest peaks in the United States, 17 are in Alaska. Of these, 11 peaks are above 15,000', but only 19 of the state's summits exceed 14,000'.

Nevertheless, Alaska can still boast some superlatives. The St. Elias Mountains are the highest coastal mountains in the world. The St. Elias and other coastal ranges also have large amounts of glacial ice, including the Malaspina Glacier, bigger than the state of Rhode Island. Five percent of Alaska is covered by glaciers, most of this ice concentrated near the south-central and southeast coastlines where moist air masses meeting the mountain barriers drop tons of snow each year. For example, Thompson Pass just north of Valdez recorded 974.5" (more than 81') of snow in a single season. The farther north you go in Alaska, the less glacial ice you encounter. The Brooks Range has very few glaciers, the largest no more than six miles in length. Light snowfall characterizes this arctic region due to very frigid winter temperatures that limit the air's ability to absorb moisture. This, combined with the vast distance from oceanic air masses, results in a polar desert climate.

Such climatic differences are not surprising given the vast size of the state—2.2 times the size of Texas. Alaska is 2,700 miles wide, nearly the distance from San Francisco to New York. From north to south it measures 1,400 miles, about the same distance as between San Diego and Seattle. In total area, Alaska equals the 21 smallest states put together!

To most outsiders, Alaska is a state that lies far north somewhere near the North Pole. While it is indeed closer to the pole than the rest of the United States, it is no farther north than much of northern Europe. Ketchikan lies at the same latitude as Dublin, Ireland or Hamburg, West Germany and Anchorage is only slightly north of Oslo, Norway. Although most Americans think of Hawaii as the westernmost state, Honolulu is at the same longitude as Bristol Bay, and some Alaskan communities, including Nome, are actually farther west. Part of the Aleutian chain crosses the 180th meridian into the eastern hemisphere, and the International Dateline must jog westward to prevent part of Alaska from being a day ahead of the rest of the state. Attu, the westernmost major island in the

Facing page: Sunset behind the Fairweather Mountains at Bartlett Cove, Glacier Bay National Park.
TOM BEAN

Maine. Indeed, the climate of Alaska does vary nearly as much as these two extremes. Climate conditions are influenced by the proximity of water and mountains. The water, acting as a huge heat sink, moderates temperature extremes of adjacent land areas. Major mountain masses, such as the Alaska Range, block the flow of warm oceanic air masses into the Interior and also keep Arctic fronts from penetrating the coastal zones.

Bathed by the warm Japanese Current, many southern Alaska coastal areas have a maritime climate similar to that of Seattle, with heavy precipitation and mild temperatures. The coldest temperature *ever* recorded for Amchitka Island in the Aleutian Islands is 16°, which is 9° warmer than Pensacola, Florida's record low. And other coastal communities such as Ketchikan have recorded temperatures below zero only on a few occasions. The January average temperature at Ketchikan is 34°, 2° warmer than the January average for New York City, which lies at a much more southerly latitude. Even Anchorage's January average of 13° is no colder than the average in places like northern Vermont, and considerably warmer than many of the Midwest and Great Plains states. While the ocean tends to keep winter temperatures within a bearable range, it also keeps the nearby land cooler in the summer. The warmest temperature ever recorded at Homer on the waterbound Kenai Peninsula is 80°. Even Anchorage, sheltered somewhat by encircling mountains but nevertheless sitting on an inland arm of the sea, Cook Inlet, has a record high of only 85°.

The vast region of Interior Alaska, drained by the Yukon River, sheltered from the moderating influence of the ocean by the Brooks Range to the north and the Alaska Range to

Aleutian chain, sits at the same longitude as the south island of New Zealand!

The great north-to-south distance means considerable variation in the lengths of day and night within the state. A common fallacy held by many outsiders is that Alaska is one cold, dark place for months at a time in winter and the opposite in summer with the sun never dropping below the horizon. This is only partially true, depending upon location. Point Barrow, along the Arctic Coast, has the longest night in the state. Sunset is on November 18 and sunrise comes on January 24. But Point Barrow's darkness is balanced by the summer sunlight, with the sun rising on May 10 and not setting again until August 2, providing 84 days of continuous daylight. By the time you get as far south as Anchorage, though, the maximum summer daylight is 19$\frac{1}{2}$ hours. Even on the shortest days of the year, Anchorage residents do, in fact, have sunlight—five and a half hours of it!

Spread over a region as vast as the entire lower 48 states, Alaska naturally has varied climates. It would be as incorrect to imply that the whole state has one climate as it would be to say the climate of all the contiguous states is as warm as Yuma, Arizona or as cold as Caribou, the south, has the greatest temperature extremes. Places like Fairbanks, Tok and Northway fit the conventional image of Alaska—cold, very cold, in winter. It is here where the frigid temperatures of 60° and 70° below zero are occasionally reported, and the record low for the entire United States, 81° below zero, was recorded on January 23, 1971 at Prospect Creek along the south slope of the Brooks Range. Strange as it may seem to some, the Interior also holds Alaska's record high— 100° recorded at Fort Yukon.

The proximity of water and mountains also affects annual precipitation. The coastal areas are the wettest, particularly those coastal areas banked by high mountains. Within Alaska's borders are some of the rainiest spots in the nation. Little Port Walter in Southeast Alaska has an annual average precipitation of 224", while MacLeod Harbour on Montague Island in Prince William Sound recorded 332" of precipitation in 1976—an average of nearly an inch per day!

Mountains influence this rainfall pattern considerably. Moist air masses from the ocean must rise to pass over mountain barriers and, in doing so, they cool. Most of their moisture condenses and falls as snow or rain. Whittier, on Passage Canal, lies at the windward base of the Chugach Mountains. Each year the nearby peaks wring an average of 175" of precipitation from the passing clouds. Anchorage, only 20 miles away but on the lee side of the Chugach Mountains, receives a mere 14" of precipitation per year.

Cold air temperatures also influence annual precipitation. The colder the air, the less moisture it can hold. Thus regions with very low average temperatures, such as the North Slope and Interior reaches of the Yukon River Valley,

tend to have a surprisingly low annual precipitation. Point Barrow lies in a cold desert zone where average annual precipitation is only 5". In 1935 only 1.6" fell on Barrow, making it as dry as Death Valley. You would not guess from the lushness of the vegetation, but communities like Fairbanks with a 10" average, and Fort Yukon with a 7" average, have less annual precipitation than Tucson, where annual average precipitation is 12" to 14". Arizona seems drier because of a much higher evaporation rate. Alaska's low evaporation rate, combined with the poor drainage resulting from underlying permafrost, makes most of the state a mire in summer.

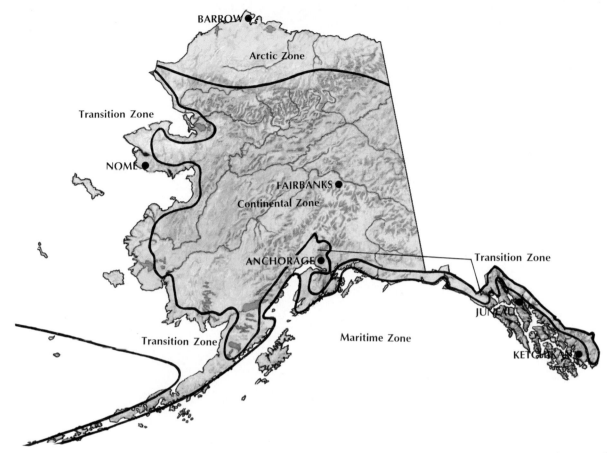

Above: Alaska's major climate zones. LINDA COLLINS
Facing page: Anchorage. GEORGE WUERTHNER

With two oceans (Pacific and Arctic) and three major seas bordering the state, there is no shortage of anchorages along its 33,904 miles of coastline. Although other states may brag about their beaches, Alaska can claim more—in fact 50 percent more—seacoast than all the rest of the United States put together.

Inland are 12 major river systems, with the 1,875-mile-long Yukon providing a navigable corridor into the heart of the state. These rivers, coupled with nearly 3 million lakes, give one the sense that Alaska is more water than land. Anyone who has flown over the Yukon Delta or the North Slope (you would not want to try walking except in winter when it is frozen) can testify that some parts of Alaska are indeed more water than land!

Anchorage, where half the state's population resides, often shocks first-time visitors by its size. This sprawling community, resting in a bowl beneath the Chugach Mountains, has its share of high-rises built of steel and glass. Beautiful parks, bike paths and ski trails lace Anchorage together, but it also has an unfinished look, with yards still largely dirt, trash-lined chain-link fences and mobile home parks seemingly placed at random among shopping malls and warehouses.

It is a common joke here to say that Anchorage is only a half hour away from Alaska. In essence this is true, as it is true of any Alaskan community. No matter how humans have degraded the natural environment, the impacts seem lost in the vastness of the land. The difference between Alaska and the rest of the nation is the closeness of wilderness. In the lower 48 states, civilization surrounds tiny patches of wilderness; in Alaska, wilderness surrounds the small areas influenced by humanity. You do not enter a wilderness area in Alaska; you go out into the bush. Of the 375 million acres that make up Alaska, one estimate claims only 160,000 acres actually have been altered by human settlement, industry and agriculture. (This figure does not count areas logged.)

Perhaps because of the severe climate and the rugged land, Alaskans tend to huddle together in villages or cities. The state's population is largely urban (64.5%), but in 1985 there were only four communities with populations greater than 5,000 people: Anchorage Borough (230,000), Fairbanks-North Star Borough (72,747), Juneau Borough (26,270) and Ketchikan Gateway Borough (12,248). These four account for 73 percent of Alaska's total population. More than 50 percent of Alaskans live in Anchorage, or the "Big Village" as some Alaskans call their largest city. Whites dominate the urban areas like Fairbanks and Anchorage, while most of the outlying communities beyond the state's highway system are populated by Alaskan Indians, Eskimo or Aleut.

Although most of the smaller villages are beyond the state's road system, few are genuinely isolated. Daily plane and mail service reaches most communities and not one Alaskan village lacks television or phone service. Even the log cabin has given way to pre-fab housing, which makes some villages look more like transplanted suburbs of Los Angeles than rustic outposts of civilization.

Right: *The mild climate and lush vegetation of Southeast Alaska belie the image many outsiders have of the state.*
GEORGE WUERTHNER
Top: *At Crow Creek Mine in the Chugach Mountains.*
JEFF GNASS
Facing page: *The rugged, granite spires of the Arrigetch Peaks in the Brooks Range were carved by Ice Age glaciers.*
GEORGE WUERTHNER

GEOLOGY

Rocks. We tend to think of them as indestructible. "Solid as granite," the saying goes. And, except for an occasional earthquake, we never think of the earth as moving or changing. It is difficult to think of continents drifting about the globe, or of glacial ice heavy enough to depress the earth's surface hundreds of feet—and perhaps even harder to believe that the earth would rebound like a rubber band. Rocks like a rubber band? Certainly not the rocks we fell on as kids, we want to say: no bounce in those things.

Understanding geology requires a different frame of reference, one encompassing not just a childhood but millions of years. Major shifts in rock position do occur, but seldom overnight.

These ideas were brought home to me years ago while I was hiking in the Wrangell Mountains. I came upon rock that looked like coral. Coral grows only in warm tropical seas. I knew a little about geology—enough to know that the rocks of today's mountain peaks often were once the bottoms of ancient seas, so I quite naturally assumed that the presence of coral on top of mountains near the Arctic Circle indicated that the entire region once had been much warmer and tropical seas had lapped against Alaskan beaches. I was partially correct. Indeed, the rocks making up the mountain I was standing upon were formed in warm tropical oceans, but not in seas anywhere near the Arctic Circle or even present-day Alaska. The limestone in the Wrangells formed in a shallow, warm sea as a coral reef growing around old volcanic islands near the equator, such as you might find today in Hawaii. Over millions of years, the chain of volcanic islands sank and eventually rose again as they were rafted northwards to their present position, then grafted on to Alaska.

The crust now fastened to Alaska as part of the Wrangell Mountains is just one piece of a giant jigsaw puzzle which makes up the upper mantle of the globe. The individual pieces constantly move relative to each other, rafted about by convection currents of molten rock formed by radioactive decay deep in the earth. Where molten rock (magma) rises toward the surface of the mantle, cracks develop, usually on the ocean floor, and new oceanic crust is formed as the magma flows outward. This is happening now in the mid-Atlantic.

Where ocean plates collide with continental plates, the oceanic material, usually of a denser, heavier rock than the more buoyant continental crust, will dive beneath the latter, forming deep oceanic trenches—as is occurring today along the edge of Alaska's Aleutian Islands. The subducting plate margin will melt into magma.

Magma, lighter than the surrounding rocks, tends to rise toward the earth's surface, where it occasionally flows out as volcanic eruptions. When it does, we call the resulting rock rhyolite, andesite or basalt depending upon its chemical properties. In Alaska the line of volcanos in the Aleutians marks a subduction zone where magma is being produced and rising to the surface. If the magma is unable to reach the surface, it cools in place under the crust, forming granitic rocks. Most granitic bodies never are seen since they lie buried beneath thousands of feet of rock. But occasionally, erosion peels away the cap rocks, exposing the granite beneath.

Facing page: Crater Lake inside Mt. Katmai. The glaciers inside the caldera are unique, since scientists know their exact age: they have formed since Mt. Katmai exploded in 1912.
WALT ANDERSON

Granite is a very hard rock that resists weathering and as a result often forms dramatic peaks. Some of the more spectacular mountains in Alaska are granitic in nature, including the Arrigetch Peaks of the Brooks Range, Denali and Ruth Gorge in the Alaska Range, and parts of the Chugach Mountains, Talkeetna Mountains, Coast Range and many others.

Mineralization is common along the margins of granitic batholiths. The tremendous heat associated with rising magma, in combination with water, dissolves minerals into solution, concentrating them from the surrounding rock. Then, as the solution cools, or the water is driven off, the precipitated minerals form veins and lode deposits. It is more than coincidental that many Alaskan gold mines are located in or near the edges of granitic outcrops.

The force of colliding plates sometime buckles the earth, forming mountains. Alaska is being squeezed from both north and south. The Pacific Plate, which is sliding under Alaska along the South-Central portion of the state, may be the force lifting the Alaska Range so high, particularly in the Mt. McKinley region. The collision of plate material from the south along the Gulf Coast near Yakutat has raised the lofty St. Elias Mountains.

The Brooks Range is a piece of earth's crust that broke off from North America 200 million years ago and rotated counter-clockwise away from the Arctic Islands in Canada so as to rest against the growing Alaska land mass. Then compressed by plate collision, it raised the mountains.

Much of the rock that presently makes up Alaska, including the limestone I encountered in the Wrangells, is composed of terranes, blocks of the earth's crust formed elsewhere. Some rocks are very similar to those now found in Asia, the South Pacific and South America. Others seem related to rocks found elsewhere in North America. They could have begun as sedimentary rocks such as sandstone, or limestone formed as accumulation basins of ancient seas or as volcanic rock erupted on the earth's surface. Whatever their origins, these blocks were rafted to Alaska, with faults separating them into narrow strips. Each new terrane was grafted onto the edge of the growing continental mass. Part of the complexity of Alaska's geology is that it is made up by as many as 50 of these narrow terrane strips.

Imagine holding a piece of clay. Then take another piece, perhaps of a different color, and push it onto the original piece. Add another layer. And another. Eventually you have a series of layers of various thicknesses and colors—terranes. The break marking each new layer represents a fault.

As a rule, the oldest rocks are found in Interior of Alaska and most subsequent additions come from the south. The various terranes are named for the areas where they were studied. The oldest rock in the Interior of Alaska along the Yukon River is called the Yukon-Tanana terrane. Grafted onto this rock slightly south and to the east is the Stikine terrane, named for the Stikine River. Slapped onto the Stikine terrane is the Tracy Arm terrane, named for a glacial fiord in the Coast Range. Slightly younger still is the Alexander terrane, which makes up most of the Alexander Archipelago. And so it goes, each terrane representing a sliver of some former continental crust that was driven northwards and slapped on to Alaska.

Some of the oldest rocks in Alaska are found along the upper Yukon and Tanana River, part of the Yukon-Tanana terrane. They formed 600 to 800 million years ago as deposits of mud and sand along the margin of North America, which then was perhaps 150 or more miles inland—along what is now the Rocky Mountains. These sedimentary deposits hardened to become sandstones, mudstones and shales. Later they were metamorphosed by heat and pressure into micaceous quartzite and graphitic schist. At the time of their original formation, the land of Alaska did not even exist. But by the time Alaska began to take shape, some 200 million years ago, these rocks drifted northward to become one of the foundations of the Alaska land mass.

The first pieces of what later would be Alaska were added onto the North American continent about 200 million years ago. At this time, North America was joined with Europe, Africa and South America in a supercontinent known as Pangaea. About 180 million years ago, Pangaea began to break up, with North America eventually separating from Europe and later from South America as it moved north and west. The North American Plate began to override the Pacific Plate.

At this time, the terranes that would be grafted onto Alaska still were offshore. But by early Jurassic time, about 180 million years ago, the Stikine terrane was docked onto Alaska, to be followed by the Alexander and Wrangellia terranes. The collision of these terranes allowed intrusions of granite to form what now is called the Coast Range batholith. A batholith is a huge body of granite formed deep in the earth, subsequently uplifted and exposed by erosion.

Approximately 65 million years ago the Chugach terrane collided with Alaska and resulted in the formation of volcanos inland.

Above: Nabesna Glacier betlow Mt. Blackburn in the Wrangell Mountains. GEORGE WUERTHNER
Left: The Tusk in Lake Clark National Park, carved by parallel glaciers grinding at each side of the spire. CHARLIE CRANGLE
Top: Major volcanic peaks. LINDA COLLINS
Facing page: Katmai erupting in 1912. M. HORNER PHOTO, MUSEUM OF HISTORY AND INDUSTRY, SEATTLE

Above: Rumble and rock debris imbedded in the bottom of a glacier act like a giant file to smooth and carve the bedrock over which the ice rides, as seen here at Yale Arm in the Chugach Mountains.
Right: Glaciers advance and retreat due to changing climatic conditions. Approximately 4,000 years ago, advancing ice buried this forest with a moraine that subsequently was excavated by erosion after the glacier retreated again. Here Al Sanders examines one of these recently-uncovered "fossil forests" at Muir Inlet in Glacier Bay National Park.
GEORGE WUERTHNER PHOTOS
Facing page: Major glaciers and ice fields. LINDA COLLINS

During the millions of intervening years these volcanos eroded away, but the underlying pool of magma, which had cooled in place as granite, now comprises the rocks of the Talkeetna Mountains.

The next drifting piece of crust to wash onto Alaskan shores was the Prince William terrane, which arrived approximately 42 million years ago. Today its rocks make up the islands of Prince William Sound.

It would be incorrect to assume that any particular terrane was made up of one primary kind of rock. Terranes are hodgepodges of different materials, reflecting their various origins. For example, the Stikine terrane includes the volcanic rocks rhyolite, andesite and basalt interbedded with sedimentary rocks like limestone, sandstone and shales In addition, the rocks of a particular terrane may be fragmented into pieces that crop out now and again over a great distance. For example, the rocks of the Wrangellia terrane can be found in the Alaska Range near Cantwell, through the Wrangell Mountains, then southward through the western islands of Southeast Alaska, down into the Queen Charlotte Islands, on Vancouver Island, and in the mountains of Idaho.

And so, piece by piece, terranes have been tacked onto Alaska, with the latest arrival the Yakutat terrane. Riding the Pacific Plate on its collision with the North American Continental Plate, this terrane is being pushed at a rate of $2^1/_2''$ per year onto Alaska, creating numerous earthquakes and driving up the St. Elias Mountains in the process. Geologists believe the Yakutat block was broken off the edge of the continent near Chatham Strait in Southeast Alaska. In its 25-million-year-long journey, it has moved 330 miles northwest.

This migration of earth's crust helps explain the presence of hydrocarbons such as coal and oil in Alaska. Coal and oil burn because they are organic, composed of matter that once was living. The vast amounts of organic matter necessary to produce coal and oil can form only in warm climates. Hence most of Alaska's hydrocarbon reserves formed when the land was farther south with a more favorable climate.

Few people realize that Alaska's North Slope contains not only one of the largest oil deposits yet discovered anywhere on earth—Prudhoe Bay—but also the largest coal province in the world. About half the United States' reserves of coal are found in Alaska and 80 percent of these deposits are found in the Naval Petroleum Reserve of Northwest Alaska on the North Slope and in the northern foothills of the Brooks Range. Other coal deposits include the Nenana field, presently being mined near Healy; the Kaltag-Galena area along the lower Yukon; near Chicken on the Fortymile River; along the Kobuk River; along the Koyukuk River near Bettles; on the Seward Peninsula; in the Cook Inlet region; Mantanuka Valley; Broad Pass in the Alaska Range; Bering River east of Cordova; Robinson Mountains near Yakutat; on the Alaskan Peninsula near Chignik and in Southeast Alaska on Admiralty, Prince of Wales and Kupreanof islands.

While the Prudhoe Bay and Cook Inlet oil fields are well known, more than half of Alaska has promising hydrocarbon-bearing basins. These areas, due to their geologic structure and rock characteristics, are known or considered candidates for oil or gas production. They include the Bristol Bay region, Gulf of Alaska, Copper River Basin, Yukon Flats-Kandik River Basin, Koyukuk Basin, Selawik Basin, Bethel Basin and Norton Sound Basin. Since some of these deposits are located in offshore basins, development would pose extremely high environmental hazards, especially in areas rich in marine resources such as salmon fisheries. But due to high extraction costs, it may be a long time before these mineral resources are developed.

As continents joined together and fell apart, and terranes came and went, world-wide climatic changes occurred also. The Ice Age of the not-too-distant past was only one of many cycles of global warming and cooling.

Most evidence for previous ice ages or warming trends has been lost due to erosion and

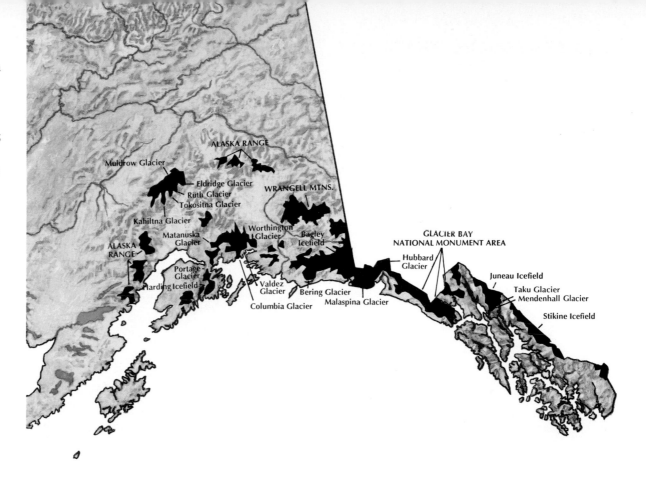

the transformation of rocks. The most recent climatic changes for which we have good evidence occurred during the Tertiary period, about 35 million years ago. At this time the climate of Alaska and the whole world was milder and warmer: desert-like conditions prevailed in the Rockies, and Alaska had a climate more temperate than today's.

This changed dramatically about 13 million years ago when glaciers began to develop in Alaska's coastal mountains. Glaciation has continued to the present, but it last peaked during the Pleistocene or Great Ice Age. The

Pleistocene began approximately 2 million years ago and included a number of glacial advances and retreats, with the last major advance, the Wisconsin Glaciation, ending only between 10,000 and 15,000 years ago. At its maximum nearly 50 percent of Alaska was sheathed in ice, while today less than 5 percent is ice-covered.

Since the Wisconsin Glaciation, there have been a few minor advances, the most recent between 1500 and 1920 A.D. and often referred to as the Little Ice Age. Because of this frequent glaciation, only the lowest of Alaska's mountains escaped some glacial sculpting.

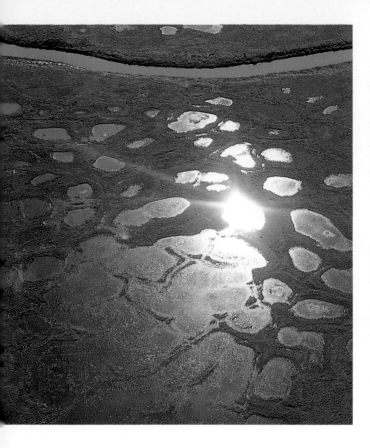

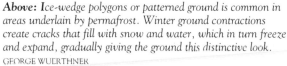

Above: Ice-wedge polygons or patterned ground is common in areas underlain by permafrost. Winter ground contractions create cracks that fill with snow and water, which in turn freeze and expand, gradually giving the ground this distinctive look.
GEORGE WUERTHNER
Right: *The Savage River Valley in Denali National Park.*
JEFF GNASS

Today glacial ice is concentrated near the Gulf of Alaska, where high mountains next to the sea catch a tremendous amount of snow. The Chugach Mountains have the most glacial ice, followed by the St. Elias Mountains, Alaska Range, and Wrangell, Coast and Kenai mountains. The Talkeetna Mountains sandwiched between the Alaska Range and the Chugach Mountains also have substantial glaciers. Much smaller glaciers dot mountain basins in the Aleutian Islands, along the Alaskan Peninsula and in the Brooks Range from the headwaters of the Noatak nearly to the Yukon border. Tiny glaciers are found in a few other mountain areas including some of the islands of the Alexander

Archipelago, Kodiak Island, Kilbuk and Wood River mountains, and on the Seward Peninsula.

During the height of glaciation, so much water was locked up in glacial ice that the world's oceans were lowered by 400′. This drop exposed the floor of the Bering Sea, allowing people to trek from Asia to North America.

Despite widespread glacial ice, much of the Interior of Alaska never was glaciated. As a result it acted as a refugia for plants and animals. The Interior valleys along the Yukon River, surrounded by high, rain-catching mountains to the south, were essentially a dry, cold steppe. Pollen research shows almost no trees—the spruce and paper birch now common were absent then. The plants found on this steppe environment were nutrient-rich and high in protein, and supported a large assemblage of Ice Age animals. Some of the mammals once common here are extinct, like the wooly mammoth. Others, like the lion, yak, camel and Saiga antelope now live only in Asia. Others disappeared from Alaska but survived in other parts of North America—like the bison, for example. Finally there are Ice Age species that still inhabit Alaska, including Dall sheep, caribou and moose. Following these Ice Age mammals was another mammal with considerable predation skills—the human.

The most recent glacial maximum occurred about 20,000 years ago, after which glaciation began a slow retreat. Approximately 6,000 to 7,000 years ago, the amount of glacial cover was at a minimum due to a world-wide warming trend, which melted icepacks and raised ocean levels. Marine terranes can now be found in various areas of Southeast Alaska, some several hundred feet above the present ocean level.

With the unloading of the ice's weight, the earth's surface began to rebound. In places this rebound measured several inches per year. I discovered this rebound vividly once while kayaking Glacier Bay. My topographic maps showed that a narrow passageway existed between Gilbert Island and the mainland in Hugh Miller Inlet. Nevertheless, when I arrived there, I found that a low isthmus now connected the island to the mainland. My maps were not incorrect—when they were made. But in the 25 years since the map had been printed, isolastic rebound had uplifted the earth by several feet, requiring me to portage.

Although glaciers may rearrange the landscape dramatically, frost—working on a smaller, slower scale—still influences Alaska's geology. Where permafrost underlies the surface, preventing drainage, the topsoil remains wet all summer. Saturated soil may slowly move downhill in a phenomenon called solifluction. Frost also causes trees to tilt in crazy angles forming "drunken" forests. And bedrock is pried loose to fall to the bottom of cliffs as talus slopes. Finally, frost creates the polygon patterns so prevalent on the earth of the North Slope and elsewhere.

EARTHQUAKES

Lying at the seam where the Pacific Plate is ramming into the North American Plate along the Alaskan Peninsula and Gulf of Alaska, Alaska is the most seismically active state in the union. Ten earthquakes between 1899 and 1986 exceeded or equaled a magnitude of 8 on the Richter scale and more than 70 quakes measured least 7 or more in magnitude.

The 1964 Earthquake, which devastated Anchorage, Valdez and other Alaskan communities, registered 8.6 on the Richter Scale—the strongest earthquake ever recorded in North America and 80 times the force that struck San Francisco in 1906. The quake and resulting seismic waves killed 131 people, 31 of them at Valdez.

Above: Devastation in Anchorage after the 1964 Alaska Earthquake. ROY CONNERS
Top: In the seismically-active Denali Range. KENNAN WARD

19

VEGETATION

On my first trip to Alaska I entered the state on the Taylor Highway coming from Dawson City in the Yukon Territory. One of my more vivid impressions came at the elevated viewpoint of Mt. Fairplay, from which a vast sweep of forest marched southwest to the Alaska Range some 60 or 70 miles away, an overwhelming impression of limitless forest. At least one third of Alaska is tree-covered. Because of the state's size, this amounts to 119 million acres of timbered country—an area larger than the entire state of California!

Spreading over 106 million acres of Alaska's Interior regions is what is called the Interior forest community. Adapted to the continental climate of cold winters and warm summers, the Interior forest community is sometimes called the northern boreal forest, or taiga, which describes a mixture of dense, well developed forest stands interspersed with open, treeless bogs, or muskegs. The warmer, better-drained slopes are dominated by white spruce, aspen, paper birch and balsam poplar, while black spruce and, to a lesser extent, eastern larch are the common species of the colder, wetter sites. Associated with the white spruce-hardwood forest are crowberry, prickly rose, buffaloberry, high bush cranberry and narrow-leaf Labrador tea. Species found on black spruce sites include sphagnum moss, Labrador tea, resin birch, shrubby cinquefoil, crowberry, cranberry and bog blueberry.

These Interior forests are found across the lower-elevation areas of the upper Yukon and Kuskokwim drainages, and in isolated belts along the narrow floodplain zone along the Kobuk and lower Noatak, lower Kuskokwim and Yukon rivers. Despite its name, the Interior forest also reaches the coast in rainshadow areas such as the upper Cook Inlet region, and on the lee side of the Alaskan Peninsula near Bristol Bay as far south as King Salmon.

Alaska's coastal forests consist of an evergreen temperate rainforest. Covering a much smaller region and making up only 13 million acres of Alaska's forested landscape, they nevertheless comprise the majority of the state's commercial timberlands. With mild temperatures and abundant precipitation, these forests grow relatively quickly. Considering the state's northern location, individual trees may attain a surprisingly large size—some Sitka spruce reach heights of 225′ and may be 10′ in diameter! These coastal forests extend from the islands of Southeast Alaska along the Gulf Coast, through Prince William Sound to Kodiak Island and the lower Cook Inlet region as far south as Kamishak Bay near Lake Iliamna.

In Southeast Alaska, the predominant species are Sitka spruce and western hemlock, with smaller amounts of mountain hemlock, Alaska cedar, western red cedar, Pacific silver fir and subalpine fir, although the last two are rather uncommon. Black cottonwood, including the world's record tree—32′ in circumference, found near Haines—are common in coastal mountain river bottoms. Lodgepole pine is common in muskeg areas—wet sites dominated by a boggy mattress of mosses, grasses and sedges. This forest community changes as one

Facing page: Autumn color in the Yukon Highlands. The spruce-hardwood forest consists of white and black spruce mixed with deciduous paper birch, aspen and balsam poplar. It covers more the 100 million acres in Alaska's Interior.
GEORGE WUERTHNER

moves west along the Gulf, with many species disappearing. Beyond Prince William Sound only mountain hemlock and Sitka spruce remain and, by the time you reach Kodiak Island, Sitka spruce is the only tree species found. Sitka spruce is apparently expanding its range southward on Kodiak Island at a rate of about one mile per century. Common plant species associated with this coastal forest include Sitka alder, salal, rusty menzeisia, devil's club, salmonberry, high bush cranberry and several species of blueberry. Of course, not all these species will inhabit every nook of the coastal forest.

In the Interior of Alaska and along the coast, a shrub zone often lies between the upper limits of tree growth and the alpine tundra. Along the coast, this zone tends to be dominated by several species of alder and willow, while in the drier Interior resin birch is often present also.

Tundra, Alaska's other major plant community, is by far its most abundant, covering half the state. From a distance, a valley filled with tundra may look like western grassland, an appealing place for a hike. But in reality, most tundra is a soggy, spongy, sodden nightmare. Hikers continuously trip over tussocks and plow through short dense thickets of dwarf shrubs.

The tundra plant community covers most of Western Alaska and the North Slope, as well as the Alaskan Peninsula and Aleutian Islands. Alpine tundra occupies a region above timberline in both the coastal forest regions of South-east and South-Central Alaska and throughout the Interior forest region south of the Brooks Range.

Moist tundra, the most common sub-set of the tundra plant community, is common in foothills and in poorly drained sites, particularly those underlain by permafrost. Often dominated by cottongrass, this plant community also may include sphagnum moss, dwarf arctic birch, resin birch, two species of mountain avens, narrow-leaf Labrador tea, alpine bearberry, alpine azalea, Lapland rosebay, mountain cranberry, a host of willow species and bog blueberry. Alpine tundra, covering the areas above timberline on many of Alaska's mountain ranges, consists of the same species as moist tundra with the exception of cottongrass and Labrador tea. Other species common to alpine tundra include diapensia, Mertens cassiope, starry cassiope and several varieties of mountain heath.

On dry ridges and gravel bars, one often encounters nearly continuous mats of dryas, a low flowering plant with tough, evergreen leaves. Lichens may be common components of the dry tundra community. Their presence usually indicates good, firm walking.

One factor that influences plant community associations is the presence or absence of permafrost. In coastal regions of the Alaskan Peninsula, Kodiak Island, the islands of Prince William Sound and Southeast Alaska, permafrost is absent, but north of Cook Inlet and the Chugach Mountains, and west of the Alaskan Peninsula near Lake Iliamna, permafrost occurs in discontinuous bands all the way to the Brooks Range. The North Slope is completely underlain by permafrost.

Any disturbance that removes the overlying cover of vegetation will allow the permafrost to melt. As this happens, ponds may form, their drainage impeded by the frozen layers beneath. Houses or other construction on permafrost must be built up off the ground, or well insulated, to prevent melting the substrate.

Permafrost influences plant growth in several ways besides impeding drainage. Permafrost limits root penetration and the availability of nutrients to the "active layer" of ground that thaws each summer. If the permafrost layer is close enough to the surface, trees cannot grow because there is not enough soil available for their root systems. Lakes and rivers act as giant thaw tanks melting the surrounding permafrost layers, which is why trees often grow in narrow bands along rivers and lakes.

Plant species reflect the distribution of permafrost. On south-facing slopes, where permafrost often is absent, grow white spruce and paper birch forests. The cooler northern exposures are dominated by the shallow-rooted black spruce and sphagnum moss.

Studies of Alaska during the period of 1898 to 1940, prior to widespread fire suppression, show that an average of 1.5 to 2.5 million acres burned annually. Scientists estimate that 54 million acres burned between the turn of the century and the early 1970s. In the past, fires typically swept through the Interior forests every 50 to 200 years. The interval is closer to 50 years in the drier forests of the upper Yukon and Porcupine drainages, and longer in the wetter western and southwest regions of the Kuskokwim and lower Yukon drainages. It is nearly impossible to find a spruce tree older than 200 years anywhere in Interior Alaska, except for an occasional stand on islands where they may have been protected from fire.

Even tundra areas burn on occasion, although in normal years tundra vegetation is

too wet to burn well. Nevertheless, there appear to be, at 50- to 100-year intervals, particularly dry summers when tundra dries sufficiently to carry fire, and thousands of acres may burn.

Plant succession after a fire often follows a predictable sequence. On the drier south-facing slopes, the burn site is invaded first by fireweed and various willow species. Both aspen and birch regenerate from their charred stumps by sprouting root suckers. If a white spruce seed

Above: *The moss-draped interior of an old-growth coastal Sitka spruce-western hemlock forest on Admiralty Island in Southeast Alaska.* GEORGE WUERTHNER
Facing page: *Storm clouds and autumn color frame a pond near Wonder Lake, Denali National Park.*
KENT & DONNA DANNEN

source is nearby, spruce also may invade the site, but since white spruce produces abundant seed only every 12 years or so, it may not be important in the recolonization effort. As a result of this pattern and the fire history of Interior Alaska, aspen and birch dominate the region's forests. Aspen prefers the driest, warmest slopes—usually south-facing—while birch is more likely to be found on the cooler east- and west-facing slopes.

Because neither birch nor aspen can regenerate well in shade, white or black spruce eventually replace them on a burn site, although this may take a hundred years or more.

On wet sites, the sequence is slightly different. Shallow permafrost helps to limit the fire's penetration so that, even though trees may be killed, much of the nutrient layer remains intact and recovery is rapid. Most of these cool, wet sites are dominated by black spruce, a tree with semi-serotinous (opening with heat) cones. The first year or two after a fire, black spruce drops tremendous quantities of seed. Rapid replacestand is likely.

In the Interior of Alaska, where cold, wet, acidic soils tend to impede nutrient recycling, fire is the main agent for nutrient flow through the ecosystem and for the continued maintenance of the region's forests. Once officials understood this, they replaced the previous policy of fire suppression with a zone system. Fires in areas close to villages or other habitation are immediately suppressed, but the amount of suppression gradually is reduced in ever-widening circles, until fire is allowed to burn uncontrolled. In the past, officials thought fire suppression was necessary to save valuable timber stands. But further study showed that the vast majority of fires occur in areas of tundra, bog and noncommercial timber. While land

recovers quickly from fires, the recovery from fire-fighting activities is less swift. Heavy equipment tears apart the tundra or moss protective layer covering permafrost and leaves long-lasting scars. The worst impacts from fires are not from the conflagrations themselves, but from human efforts to "save" the forests. Putting out fires destroys the important ecological process of nutrient cycling and forest regeneration.

Slow biological breakdown and nutrient cycling cause problems for the plants in the tundra ecosystem. One means of adaptation is quite obvious to the casual observer—tundra plants are dwarfed, growing close to the ground. Since shading is not a problem on the treeless tundra, there is no need for a plant to invest in stems and stalks. But a tundra plant can't scrimp on energy investment for flowers or roots. Thus, tundra plants often have outlandishly large blooms in proportion to overall plant size. Roots, essential for gathering the limited nutrients and moisture available, also are not compromised. Relative to the overall size of the plant, many tundra species have large root areas and plants devote most of the first few years of growth to root development. The root system also stores most of the plant's yearly accumulation of excess energy.

But even with lower energy demands provided by the plant's dwarf stature, most tundra plants cannot store enough excess energy in a single season to flower. It may take three to five years for a plant to accumulate sufficient carbohydrate stores to produce a single flower. This is one reason biologists say that the tundra is extremely fragile—the difference between success and failure is very slim.

Micro-habitats influence tundra plant forms. Windswept hilltops and ridges are among the more extreme micro sites where drought, soil frost action and wind abrasion all are problems. Most vegetation in these sites tend to be small, dwarfed, cushion- or rosette-like plants. Their compact shape and the shield created by outer leaves protect the growing center from wind abrasion and also help to slow wind velocity over the leaf surfaces, thus reducing evaporation.

Drought is a common problem for many tundra plants despite the soggy nature of the land. Soils may be frozen much of the year, making it impossible for a plant to replace water lost through evaporation. Evergreen leaves are more efficient in water conservation, so not surprisingly, many tundra plants, like dryas, moss campion and purple mountain saxifrage, have evergreen leaves.

Above: The brilliant color of wild geraniums graces Alaska. *Left:* Lousewort and cow parsnip in the Kenai Mountains. ERWIN & PEGGY BAUER PHOTOS

Facing page: Fire is a natural agent for recycling nutrients in Interior forests, where wet, cold, acidic soils hinder the biological breakdown of plant litter. After fire burns an area *(top),* pioneering deciduous species like aspen or birch *(bottom right)* invade the site, but these shade-intolerant species eventually are replaced by evergreen species like the white spruce *(bottom left).* GEORGE WUERTHNER PHOTOS

Plants with evergreen leaves gain another advantage in the spring, since they can begin photosynthesizing as soon as warm temperatures arrive, while deciduous plants first must grow new leaves. In the short arctic summer, even a delay of a few weeks may mean the difference between survival and failure.

Despite their advantages, evergreen leaves are energy-expensive to produce and usually less efficient in terms of maximum photosynthetic rates than deciduous leaves. Hence, where drought and growing seasons are not problems, plants with deciduous leaves still have advantages over evergreens.

Many tundra plants avoid drought by growing in hollows or behind rocks where lingering snow cover protects them from wind abrasion and drought.

Low temperature also affects the tundra environment, and most arctic plants are adapted genetically for growth at colder temperatures. In addition to their low profile, the often-dark color of leaves and petals helps to absorb solar radiation, increasing the temperature inside the plant as much as 10° or more above the ambient air temperature.

Predictably, most tundra plants are frost-hardy and can tolerate occasional periods of below-zero temperatures without harm.

Tundra plants also have several strategies for pollination. In the windy, cold arctic, only the hardiest of insects can pollinate. The bumble-bee's large size allows it to hold heat better than, say, the smaller honeybee (which is not found here), as well as to fly in the often-high winds. Flies are among the most important tundra plant pollinators. They fly well in high winds and their dark bodies absorb solar radiation even on cool days. Different flowers are adapted for specific pollinators. For example, because of differences in the insects' mouth parts, small, flat flowers are typically "fly flowers," while long-tubed ones are typically visited by bumblebees. Many tundra flowers have a parabolic shape with dark center to focus heat toward the middle of the bloom. Pollination by insects that alight on the flower to soak up heat thus is likely to occur.

Plants have several strategies for seed dispersal. Some, like the blueberry, hide their seeds in edible fruits, and the seeds are scattered over the countryside after being eaten by birds, grizzlies or humans. Others, like the dryas and dwarf fireweed, produce light, feathery seeds that winds carry great distances. Still other plants produce a seed capsule perched upon a stiff stalk that protrudes above the snow. In winter during the frequent wind storms, the capsule cracks and the stiff stalk vibrates in the wind like a rattle. The seeds shake loose and are blown across the snow.

Left: Tussock growth on the wet tundra. As the center of the plant grows, dead leaf material gradually builds up on the sides, shading out other plants. Eventually a tussock may grow three feet high. Walking over such ground is a humbling experience: one either balances atop the tussocks or trips walking between them.
Right: A typical coastal muskeg bog on a poorly drained site.
GEORGE WUERTHNER PHOTOS

GLACIAL SUCCESSION

Plant succession after a glacier's retreat has been studied at Glacier Bay and elsewhere. The sequence and species of trees and shrubs may differ according to distance from the coast, but the principle is similar. The first plant to colonize glacial rubble is dryas (mountain avens). Its mat-like growth helps to hold loose soil in place, slowing erosion and building up soil organic levels.

After 25 to 30 years, the shrub Sitka alder will establish itself on the dryas mat. Alder takes in atmospheric nitrogen and makes it useable by other plants. The nitrogen provided by the alder improves soil-nutrient levels substantially. Tree species like black cottonwood become established and soon overtop the shrub, shading it out. Eventually Sitka spruce establishes itself and shades out the cottonwood. It is not uncommon to walk in the spruce forests at Glacier Bay and find old moss-draped dead snags of alder decaying in the dark understory. Finally, growing up in the understory of the Sitka spruce, the western hemlock concludes this sequence, for it can grow in its own shade. The result is a moss-strewn old-growth forest.

Top left: A mat of dryas colonizes a fresh glacial moraine at Wachusett Inlet, Glacier Bay.
Top right: Dryas flower.
Bottom left: Wild roses and poplars.
Bottom right: An open spruce forest.
GEORGE WUERTHNER PHOTOS

WILDLIFE

Nothing is more strongly associated with Alaska than its wildlife. Mention Alaska and most people immediately think of the seemingly vast herds of migrating caribou, of salmon jamming coastal streams, flocks of geese pouring through the Copper River Delta and breeding fur seals crowded on the Pribilof Islands. But as abundant as Alaska's wildlife may seem, it is a paltry example of what exists in more productive climates farther south. By comparison, California or Massachusetts could easily produce far more wildlife per acre than Alaska. In terms of productivity, Alaska's cold climate and nutrient-poor soils mean that, overall, the land's ability to produce significant numbers of any species is severely limited.

Most species are spread thinly across the land, with an occasional seasonal concentration giving the impression of abundance. While a herd of 10,000 caribou may travel through a single Brooks Range pass, in all likelihood there may not be another caribou for 50 miles in any direction. Huge flocks of birds do concentrate in Alaska during summer, but only a handful remain as year-round residents. And those huge trout one is always seeing in the fishing magazines—how do they get so large if Alaska's productivity is so limited? The answer is that those fish live to an old age due to limited fishing pressure. If the trophy waters of the Bristol Bay region endured the fishing pressure (with fish taken and not released), as occurs on the Henry's Fork River in Idaho or the Madison River in Montana, the average size would decline.

Alaska has abundant wildlife resources relative to the rest of the United States simply because most of the state is still wilderness and wildlife habitat is intact. The native people took advantage of the seasonal concentrations of wildlife, and knew that if they wanted to intercept the whale migration, or the salmon run, they had to be in a certain place at a specific time or miss out entirely. Life for Alaska's native people, just as for its wildlife, was centered around tapping the sequential abundances as they became available. The grizzlies that catch salmon during the spawning run, the birds that take advantage of the summer flush of insects, and the wolves that tail a migrating caribou herd all capitalize on the seasonal nature of the Alaskan environment, too.

Nevertheless, if you see a caribou migration, or a salmon run in its height, it is easy to forget scarcity. Camped once along the shore of Iliamna Lake during the height of the sockeye salmon run, I remember standing on a cliff watching the salmon run by. As far out from shore as I could see, nothing but a solid mass of fish moved up the lake. The migration never seemed to stop and, indeed, during the few days I was camped at this location, it did not.

Despite this apparent abundance, I knew better than to conclude that salmon are always as numerous as what I saw at Iliamna, for there is tremendous variation in numbers year to year and even week to week. Wildlife populations are anything but stable, particularly in the far north. We still do not understand all the causes for these variations and apparent cycles. The apparent four-year population boom-bust of the

Facing page: Caribou bulls challenge each other.
MARK NEWMAN; TOM STACK & ASSOCIATES

lemming and the 10-year cycles of the snow-shoe hare and lynx are some examples. But even larger mammals go through cycles or at least vary in numbers due to changes in habitat quality, climatic conditions and predation pressure, among other factors.

Moose, for example, browse. Recently-burned areas are often invaded by shrubs and brush. These in turn attract the moose, whose nutritional level is increased by the browse available. Cow moose with higher nutrition levels are more likely to produce twins and the young are healthier and more likely to survive into adulthood. As a result of massive wildfires during the early part of this century, Alaska's moose population exploded during the 1950s and early 1960s. The abundant food source coincided with a decrease in predation, since wolf control was practiced over much of Alaska.

A combination of low predation pressure and high nutrient level led to what might have been an all-time population high for Alaska's moose.

But the good times did not last. Due to the Bureau of Land Management's fire suppression activities, the acreage of woodlands that burned each year steadily declined. This resulted in less new moose habitat. Eventually, much of the shrubby habitat was replaced by trees or the shrubs simply grew tall enough to be beyond the reach of moose. The animals' nutrition levels dropped. At the same time, wolf control ended. A number of harsh winters took their toll and the weaker moose became susceptible to predation.

Alaska's wolves wasted no time in responding to this abundant, vulnerable food supply, and began to make inroads into the moose population. Moose by this time were suffering

from deteriorating habitat quality and the number of twins and the condition of young born declined dramatically.

As a coup de grace, Alaska's human population, both whites and Natives, increased substantially between the 1950s and the 1970s. Increased hunting pressure, combined with greater access provided by the widespread use of snowmobiles, outboard motorboats, airboats, airplanes and all-terrain vehicles, took its toll upon wildlife. No longer were there areas so inaccessible that few hunters penetrated them.

What happened to the wolves? Wolves, like humans and most other predators, can switch prey. A wolf pack that had been hunting moose could switch to hunting caribou and Dall sheep, and thus maintain their own numbers or at least slow their decline.

This has an unsuspected benefit. When prey species populations are kept low, the plants these animals browse can recover from heavy browsing pressure. Consequently, some conservationists believe the Alaska Fish and Game Department's decision to reinstitute wolf control is unwise. It may, in effect, lead to habitat depletion by moose, sheep, caribou, deer and other prey species due to over-utilization of range resources.

If given enough time, wolf numbers eventually will decline of their own accord as wolves eat themselves out of house and home. At some point, the prey animals become so scarce and so widely spread over the landscape that it becomes impossible for a wolf pack to get enough to eat. Then the wolves no longer breed or, if they do, the young do not survive into adulthood. The remaining wolves either move to new, unoccupied habitat where prey is still abundant—assuming that a resident wolf pack is not already there—or more likely they starve,

and the wolf population becomes locally extinct.

Local extinction of the wolf, whether naturally occurring or because of hunting by humans, has a ripple effect through the environment. Many other species depend, in part, upon the wolf for their survival. Eskimos, for example, used to watch the sky for circling ravens. The ravens follow wolves in the winter, living off their leavings. The presence of ravens meant wolves. The presence of wolves meant big game and if the hunter was lucky, meat for himself and his family. Arctic foxes also follow wolves, as do wolverines. Each of these scavengers would have a more difficult time making it through the winter without the handouts provided by wolf kills.

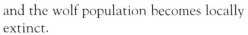

But local extinction is not unusual, especially in the Arctic. Most species are adapted to a boom-bust survival strategy. They breed rapidly when food is abundant and attempt to survive the lean times. Such was the strategy of human populations in the pre-European–contact days, but modern medicine, welfare and access to outside food resources means that people living in Alaska, even in remote bush communities, are no longer kept in balance with the available prey base—hence the need for hunting regulations and bag limits.

Another example of the interrelationship between prey, predator and plants involves the snowshoe hare cycle. Long ago the Hudson's Bay Company noticed that lynx furs followed cycles. The principal prey of the lynx is the snowshoe hare. The hare populations are cyclic. After a population crash, it is difficult to find a snowshoe hare in the woods. Gradually, their numbers grow, and since population growth is

Above: *A red fox enjoys the sun's warmth.* TOM MANGELSEN
Top: *Moose have expanded their range in Alaska.* PAT POWELL
Left: *Gray wolf.* ERWIN AND PEGGY BAUER
Facing page: *The large paws of the lynx allow it to walk easily over snow. Its cyclic population total depends on the population of its chief prey, the snowshoe hare.* ALAN D. CAREY

exponential, the population begins doubling at frequent intervals and may reach densities of 600 hares per square mile. The hare browses on willows and other plants. As the snowshoe hare population increases, the willows are progressively chewed back to thick stems. The willows, threatened with extinction themselves as a result of the severe browsing pressure, change their survival strategies. Instead of devoting energy to new growth, the plants begin to produce a toxin that discourages snowshoe-rabbit browsing. The toxin is produced only as a last resort because it takes energy the plant could use to produce seeds, leaves, roots and stems. Eventually, the snowshoe rabbits find the food unpalatable. They also have less to eat simply because of their recent over-browsing. Disease can spread through the dense population and, in their weakened condition, they easily become victims of predators like the lynx. There is a delay in the response of predators to prey abundance, so that, as the snowshoe hare population is actually on the decline, lynx numbers are still rising. Eventually the snowshoe hares' numbers decline to such a low point that lynx themselves starve.

The plants, though, relieved of browsing pressure, re-allot their energy from toxin production to new growth and quickly recover from the over-browsing. The snowshoe hare population, likewise relieved of predation pressure, responds to the high-quality, abundant food resources and begins to reproduce at a rapid rate. The cycle begins anew.

Each animal and plant has a different ecological strategy for survival and each strategy has a cost. Strategies are not something that the animal or plant obviously thinks about, but result from natural selection over thousands of years of evolution. The most obvious environ-

mental stress most Alaskan animals must endure is the cold climate.

The ability to survive cold depends on several factors. Behavior changes can allow an animal to avoid the worst cold or somehow use the environment to its advantage. In addition, what an animal eats and its body size have much to do with its ability to survive cold. As a general rule, animals with larger bodies can endure cold stress better than smaller animals. This is one reason why most mammals that are active above ground year-round tend to be big-game species like moose or caribou, while smaller mammals like the vole or lemming remain under the snow.

Smaller animals have a problem with their surface-to-volume ratio. Large animals tend to retain heat better than smaller ones because they have less surface exposed to the air, compared to their mass. The solution for small animals is to remain under the snow where its insulating quality keeps heat losses within reason. Animals such as lemmings, voles and shrews are all active in winter, but almost never leave the protective environment of the nival world—the world of snow.

The smaller the body size of the animal, the more it needs a high-quality diet in order to meet the metabolic demands of cold. Hence, a small animal like the weasel can survive the Alaskan winter only because, as a carnivore, it has a high-quality meat diet. Most vegetative matter, except buds and seeds, is low in stored energy, hence animals dependent upon leafy matter for survival must be a certain minimum size—about the size of the snowshoe hare—and have an extremely insulating coat to survive the winter.

Some vegetation-eating mammals avoid the cold altogether by adopting a slightly different

strategy: hibernation. Animals use hibernation to avoid unfavorable conditions. In the case of Alaska, that condition is winter. Two Alaskan mammals that hibernate, the marmot and ground squirrel, dine on lush plant material in summer and store fat for fuel during the long winter sleep. During hibernation, body temperature drops to just above freezing and metabolic needs drop sharply. But one of the costs of relying on this strategy is that the animal must put on sufficient fat in summer to last through an entire winter. Failure to do so may result in death. If for some reason the winter is particularly long, and the insulating snow cover is limited, marmots and ground squirrels may die in their burrows due to starvation or freezing.

The grizzly bear's survival strategy resembles those of the marmot and ground squirrel. It eats

Above: *Hoary marmots are vegetarians, colonial animals with each colony dominated by one large, old male. To avoid the rigors of the Alaska winter, they hibernate.* KENNAN WARD
Left: *Arriving as early as March to nest, golden eagles are among the earliest migrants to arrive here each year.* ALAN D. CAREY
Facing page, top: *The white Dall sheep frequents the drier mountain ranges of the state.* GEORGE WUERTHNER
Bottom left: *The cyclic numbers of snowshoe hares peak every 10 years.* PAT POWELL
Bottom right: *Brown bears on the McNeil River.* KENNAN WARD

Above: *Brown bears and grizzlies are actually the same species, but the brown bear in Alaska tends to be larger since it lives along the coastal areas where salmon fisheries provide a rich food base. The grizzly, seen here, resides in interior mountains where food is scarcer and it tends to be smaller.*
ERWIN & PEGGY BAUER
Right: *Pika.* PAT POWELL
Facing page, top: *Coyote.* KENNAN WARD
Bottom: *The ptarmigan, white in winter, turns a mottled brown in summer.* KENNAN WARD

foods rich in protein, fats and sugars all summer, attempting to store a reserve layer of fat. Bears then spend the winter in dens, to reduce their heat losses, but they are not true hibernators. Their body temperatures drop only slightly and they can be awakened from their slumbers. Bears are even known to leave their dens in mid-winter if temperatures remain high.

But even animals active all winter, like the Dall sheep, must put on a layer of fat in summer. Usually their winter diet is nutritionally insufficient to maintain body weight and they suffer a gradual loss of weight all winter. To conserve energy, many large mammals also decrease their metabolism in winter—a form of wakeful hibernation—as a means of saving energy. Studies of captive animals fed all the food they want have shown that a decrease in metabolism reduces food requirements.

Animals like Dall sheep and moose modify their behavior to take advantage of topographic conditions that help conserve heat. Since cold air sinks, sheep and moose move upslope in winter where warmer temperatures are more common. In addition, they take advantage of the limited solar energy by seeking out sheltered, south-facing slopes for wintering.

Among those animals that remain active above the snow, other adaptations help them survive the winter. While the white winter coats of the snowshoe hare, weasel, arctic fox and other species primarily camouflage those animals, there is a secondary benefit. The white hairs of these species are hollow, trapping dead air and helping to conserve heat.

Animals like the moose, deer and caribou also have hollow hairs. Besides adding insulating value, these hairs also add buoyancy—one reason these animals are capable swimmers. Some deer in Southeast Alaska have been known to swim more than five miles between islands, and moose have been spotted swimming across the 10-mile width of Glacier Bay. I once followed a swimming moose for three miles on the Yukon River.

Most of Alaska's land mammals either have special adaptations that allow them to survive the winter or they merely avoid it through hibernation. The state also has some 425 species of birds, a very high number considering the state's northern latitude and its climate. This number is explained by one of the most widely-adopted survival strategies: migration. Rather than attempt to deal with Alaska's winter climate, most birds leave, and return to Alaska only when environmental conditions are favorable for breeding and survival. Some species, such as the Arctic tern, fly nearly 22,000 miles on their migration—traveling from Antarctica to Alaska, always chasing an endless summer.

Migration is a hazardous enterprise, but it has its benefits. The mass exodus each winter creates a large number of unoccupied niches. Secondly, birds returning in summer enter Alaska during its maximum solar flush when nutrients and energy levels are high. These advantages counter the negative costs of migration.

Excepting sea birds, whose environment is relatively constant, of the birds that do remain in Alaska year-round, most have special adaptations. For example, the ptarmigan turns camouflaged white in winter. Ptarmigans also grow feathers on their feet, to protect against freezing, and the birds often dive into snowbanks during intensely cold weather, using the snow as insulation.

The raven is perhaps one of the most unusual arctic birds. It has no apparent physical adaptations. It has an extremely high metabolism, so must obtain large quantities of food to keep from freezing. But the raven survives by its wits: a good predator in its own right, it kills about half its food, and obtains the rest by scavenging kills of other predators, animals killed by vehicles, and occasionally raiding garbage dumps.

As Lois Crisler, author of *Arctic Wild*, said: "Land without wildlife is dead scenery." It is the wildlife found in Alaska's mountains that makes these mountains more than scenery—part of a vibrant ecological unit.

PEOPLE ON THE LAND

Alaska's mountains always have influenced and shaped human affairs, for they form the backdrop against which human events unfold. The mountains dictated where native people, and later the Europeans and Americans, could go, and what they could do there.

Human history in Alaska begins with the Ice Ages. At that time, Alaska's mountains were huge reservoirs of glacial ice that, along with continental glaciers formed elsewhere, lowered the world's sea level sufficiently to expose a land bridge between Asia and Alaska—a thousand miles wide. Over this tundra-steppe rangeland a host of Ice Age mammals crossed from Asia into North America. The bridge was finally breached by rising sea waters about 14,000 years ago, but even then the channel remained narrow and could be crossed on sea ice in winter.

Following the herds of wildlife were big-game hunters, the Paleo-Indians, precursors of today's North American Indians. Because the high mountains bordering the coastal areas of southern Alaska created a rainshadow, blocking the passage of moist air masses, even during maximum glacial cover the Interior valleys of Alaska were completely ice-free. Here the Paleo-Indian hunters could hunt the rich mega-fauna, including the mastodon and wooly mammoth, as well as species still present, such as moose, Dall sheep, caribou and musk ox. All these typically "Alaskan" animals owe their origins to Asian stock.

Although some fragmentary and controversial evidence suggests that humans entered North America as long ago as 30,000 years, the only conclusive evidence shows that people were in Alaska by 12,000 years ago.

Whether Alaska was continuously occupied during this diversification period is open to speculation because there is no evidence. But there is evidence that Alaska continued to be invaded by new cultural groups, each with a more advanced technology and each leaving more archaeological remains.

The last major cultural development prior to the European discovery of Alaska occurred about 1,600 years ago (400 A.D., or shortly before the beginning of the Middle Ages in Europe) when the Eskimo culture as we know it began to develop. It is not known whether this culture grew from that of an existing Alaskan group or was brought by another wave of technologically advanced people from Asia. These people were specialized in hunting sea mammals—such as whales, walruses and seals—but also relied upon fish and some land mammals like caribou. The traditional Eskimo use of dogs to pull sleds did not appear until about 1500 A.D. (about the time the first Europeans sailed to the New World); previously sleds were pulled by humans. This culture, called the Thule tradition—after Thule, Greenland—gave rise to that of the modern Eskimo. The Thule Eskimo culture spread so recently that it did not reach southern Greenland until 1200 A.D.—some 300 years *after* the Vikings established colonies there.

By the 1700s, Eskimo-Aleut people occupied Alaska's coastal regions from the Arctic southward through the Aleutians and Kodiak Island. Even Prince William Sound was Eskimo country, and the Chugach Mountains derive

Left top: Abundant food in Southeast Alaska freed time for other activities, including the artwork of carving totem poles. GEORGE WUERTHNER
Bottom: Petroglyphs in the Wrangell area. KENT KRONE
Facing page: Raw growth marked Juneau in midsummer, 1897. MUSEUM OF HISTORY AND INDUSTRY, SEATTLE

their name from the Chugach Eskimos who lived in this region.

The Eskimo culture did not spread through an uninhabited landscape. In many areas, Eskimo people directly conflicted with another major aboriginal group—the Indian people. These two groups had different survival strategies. Indians, even those living beside the sea, retained more of a land-based lifestyle than the sea-adapted Eskimos. But these groups did share and borrow ideas.

There were two major sub-sets of the Indian group. Athabascans occupied most of the middle and upper Yukon drainage, as well as upper Cook Inlet and the Copper River country, and Tlingit-Haida resided among the coastal islands of Southeast Alaska.

The Athabascans led a precarious existence based primarily on fishing the great runs of salmon along the Yukon and its tributaries,

combined with hunting. In their resource-poor and harsh land, they had to be highly mobile, which forced them to live in small family groups. Starvation was not uncommon.

The Tlingit-Haida people, on the other hand, occupied the temperate rainforests of Southeast Alaska with their rich food resources such as salmon, sea and land mammals and numerous wild plants. With a surplus of food resources, these people were able to develop a rich cultural tradition based upon the accumulation of wealth, including slaves. War was the usual means of obtaining slaves and other goods, so these people were very aggressive. Within historical times, the Tlingit were expanding their territory westward, driving out the Chugach Eskimos.

Conflicts between Eskimo and Indian were overshadowed when the next wave of humanity reached Alaska's shores. In 1741, George

Steller (for whom the Steller's sea lion and Steller's jay are named), a naturalist with a Russian exploratory expedition commanded by a Dane, Vitus Bering (for whom the Bering Sea and Bering Glacier are named), went ashore on Kayak Island near what is today Cordova—becoming the first white man known to step upon Alaskan soil. Bering had sailed up through what is now known as the Bering Strait much earlier, in 1728, but had failed even to sight land, due to poor weather conditions. The 1741 expedition was his second and last attempt to explore Alaska's shores.

After this brief contact with the North American coast, the Bering expedition sailed for Russia, but its leader did not live to complete his journey. His ship wrecked on the Commander Islands and Bering, along with a few other crew members, died that winter. The remainder of the crew built a smaller boat from the shattered remains of their vessel and returned to Russia, taking back the pelts of sea otters they had killed while trapped on the islands. The furs caught the attention of rough illiterate Russian adventurers called promyshlemniki who realized the profit potential in sea otter fur trade. The promyshlemniki swept over the Aleutian Islands, making slaves of the Aleuts and pelts of sea otters.

While the Russians were swarming over the Aleutians, other Europeans were sailing along the coast of Alaska searching not for furs but for the fabled Northwest Passage. In the process they left behind a rich legacy of place names. Six Spanish expeditions to Alaska between 1774 and 1790 left Spanish names—Valdez, Cordova, Revillagigedo—on the Alaskan map. Alaska expeditions were mounted by other European countries, including France, which sent Captain Jean La Perouse north in 1786.

(La Perouse Glacier at Glacier Bay bears his name.) But it was the English who most thoroughly explored and left the most names upon the land. Captain James Cook explored the Gulf Coast, the Aleutians and as far north as the Seward Peninsula in 1778. He named, among other landmarks, Cook Inlet, Cape Douglas near Katmai, Cape Prince of Wales on the Seward Peninsula and Prince William Sound. After Cook was killed in the Hawaiian Islands, several of his young officers came back to Alaska on expeditions of their own. These included George Dixon (for whom Dixon Entrance is named) in 1787, and George Vancouver (for whom Mt. Vancouver and Vancouver, British Columbia are named) in 1794. Vancouver, in turn, named Admiralty Island and Chatham Strait.

Despite these intrusions of other foreign powers, the Russians dominated Alaska for nearly 75 years. The rough, independent promyshlemnikis gave way to organized fur companies. With more financial muscle behind them, these companies sought to create permanent settlements, the first founded by Gregory Shelikhov at Three Saints Bay on Kodiak Island.

In 1791, the Kodiak Island settlement came under the supervision of Alexander Baranov, for whom Baranof Island in Southeast Alaska is named. Baranov eventually became manager of the Russian-American Fur Company, which obtained an exclusive charter in 1799 for the Alaska fur trade. With charter in hand, Baranov set up other Russian outposts, including New Archangel (burned in an Indian raid) near present-day Sitka, and even Fort Ross in northern California.

Sitka became the capital of Russian America and various governors lived there in relative splendor as colonial lords of a vast empire.

During this period, the Russian Orthodox Church assumed greater power, setting up schools and churches throughout Russian America. Its influence remains today in many communities throughout the old Russian colony.

While the Russians explored the coast, the British-owned Hudson's Bay Company also moved into the region, from the east. Fort Yukon, an HBC post, was established in 1847,

Above: *An Alaskan Indian couple in potlatch dancing costumes, 1906.* CASE & DRAPER PHOTO, MUSEUM OF HISTORY AND INDUSTRY, SEATTLE

Facing page: *Eskimos pose by a skin hut, where fur seals and inflated seals are drying, in 1899. Cured inflated seals served as bobbers on harpoons, helping hunters keep track of their harpoons and also causing resistance when harpooned animals attempted to dive.* EDWARD CURTIS PHOTO, MUSEUM OF HISTORY AND INDUSTRY, SEATTLE

well within Russian-claimed territory, to tap the Indian fur trade of the upper Yukon region. Other HBC employees explored the Stikine and coastal areas of Southeast Alaska, much to the dismay of the Russians.

With the 1853 outbreak of the Crimean War between Russia and Britain, apprehension grew in Russia that the British might take Alaska by force. Not wanting enemies at their back door across the Bering Sea, the Russians began secret talks with the United States about the latter's buying Russia's New World possessions.

Negotiations continued for years, but in 1867, at the urging of the American Secretary of State, William Seward (for whom the town of Seward is named), the United States offered $7,200,000 for Alaska. The Russians were quite taken aback by the offer. Unbeknownst to the Americans, the Russians had thought they would be lucky to get $5 million for Alaska and had even decided to give their colony free of charge to the United States, if necessary, to prevent it from falling under British control. Many Americans, on the other hand, thought the Russians were fools for giving up such a large chunk of real estate for such a trifling amount of money.

Of course, not all Americans felt that the purchase of Alaska was a good deal. Some called it "Seward's folly" or "Seward's icebox," but a scant five years later, the jeering stopped when gold was discovered near Sitka—with other discoveries in Southeast Alaska following in rapid succession.

The gold discoveries drew Americans northward and helped to establish Southeast Alaska as an American outpost, but the vast Interior remained virtually unknown. The federal government sent a number of military expeditions north to map this territory during

the late 1800s. The first of these was led by
Lieutenant Frederick Schwatka, for whom the
Schwatka Mountains in the Brooks Range are
named. In 1883, Schwatka floated 1,300 miles
of the Yukon River and first alerted the outside
world about the gold possibilities of the
Interior.

Between 1884 and 1886, two other military
men, George Stoney and John Cantwell, led
separate expeditions to explore the headwaters
of the Kobuk and Noatak rivers in the western
Brooks Range.

In 1885, Lieutenant Henry Allen (for whom
Allen Glacier along the Copper River and the
Allen River in the Brooks Range are named)
led a 1,500-mile-long trek across Alaska.
Allen's journey was an epic tale of starvation
and deprivation. He, along with Cady Robertson (for whom the Robertson River in the
Alaska Range is named) and Frederick Fickett,
first traveled up the Copper River where they
learned about the great copper deposits later
developed at McCarthy in the Wrangell
Mountains. Near today's Slana, they crossed
the Alaska Range and floated down the Tanana
River to the Yukon. Robertson dropped out
here, but Allen and Fickett continued overland
to the Kanuti River and thence up the Koyukuk
to the present-day Bettles area before turning
back as autumn approached.

These early explorations helped to roughly
define Alaska's major landmarks and river
systems, but it took the discovery of gold in
Alaska's Interior to fill in most of the blank
spots on the maps. Until the 1880s, most gold
prospecting had been confined to Southeast
Alaska, but early traders operating on the
Yukon and its tributaries knew that small
amounts of gold were to be found in the
Interior. However, not until 1886 and a major

placer discovery on the Fortymile River, did
hundreds of prospectors flock to the region.

After the Fortymile discovery, other placer
gold discoveries soon followed at Circle City
(1893) and Hope-Sunrise (1896), and
extremely rich placers were found on the
Klondike River in the Yukon Territory in 1896.
News of this find precipitated one of the biggest
gold rushes of all time, when an estimated
100,000 people came north in 1898. But by the
time most would-be miners arrived at Dawson
City, located at the confluence of the Yukon
and Klondike rivers, the richest claims had
already been staked.

Many of these disappointed prospectors left
the north almost as quickly as they had come,

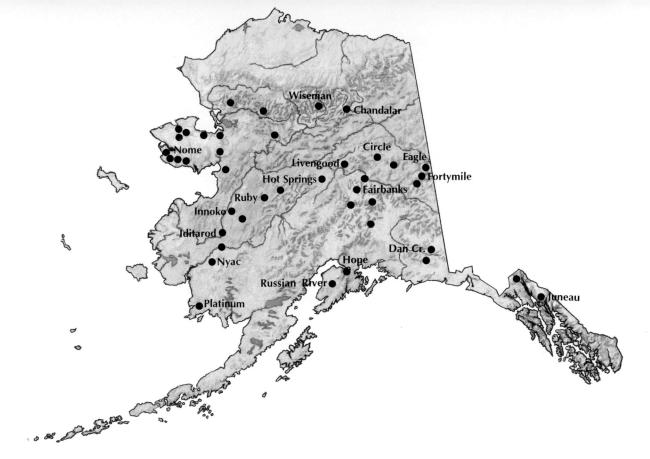

Above: The lure of gold drew thousands to Alaska and the
virtually unknown Interior was mapped primarily by miners
seeking undiscovered placers. Map shows location of major gold
camps. LINDA COLLINS

Facing page, top: The back-breaking labor of getting rich
quick at placer mining. HEGG NEG. 1767, SPECIAL COLLECTIONS,
UNIVERSITY OF WASHINGTON

Bottom left: Russian governor Alexander Baranov. SPECIAL
COLLECTIONS, UNIVERSITY OF WASHINGTON

Bottom right: Frederick Schwatka, a military explorer, floated
1,300 miles of the upper Yukon River and noted in his reports
that the Interior contained gold. SPECIAL COLLECTIONS, UNIVERSITY
OF WASHINGTON

but others spread out and roamed the rest of Alaska looking for the big find. The next one came in 1898 at Nome, but news of it did not reach Seattle until 1899. Other discoveries followed in rapid order: Fairbanks (1902), Innoko (1906), Ruby (1907), Iditarod (1908), Wiseman (1910), Marshall (1913), Chisana (1913) and Livengood (1914). The search for gold turned up other important minerals and fossil fuels, including the copper deposits in the Wrangells and coal deposits near Healy and along Cook Inlet and the Kobuk River. The first interest in Alaskan oil also emerged at this time with claims staked as early as 1891 in Cook Inlet and the first well developed by 1902 at Katalla near Cordova.

The influx of people swelled the population to more than 60,000. Alaska was granted territorial status in 1912, and allowed to send one delegate to Congress.

As the easily-worked gold placer deposits played out after the turn of the century, Alaska began to exploit its fisheries fully. In the peak year of 1936, Alaska recorded its all-time record salmon catch of 126.4 million fish. Since then the fishing industry has declined.

Alaska muddled through the Depression, perhaps in better condition than the rest of the United States, but World War II and the Cold War brought economic prosperity. At the beginning of the real war just 72,000 people lived in Alaska, only slightly more than at the turn of the century. The surprise Japanese attack on the Aleutian Islands in 1942 convinced U.S. military strategists that Alaska was important in any modern war, its northerly location making over-the-pole flights a possibility. The Alcan Highway, constructed in 1942 in nine months, sped supplies to Alaska and the military built airstrips throughout the

bush. By 1943, there were 150,000 military men stationed in Alaska and the federal government spent more than a billion dollars in the state between 1941 and 1945.

During the 1950s, the military build-up continued around Anchorage and Fairbanks. During this same period, the U.S. Forest Service decided to promote Alaska's timber industry to create jobs in Southeast Alaska. Several major pulp and timber mills were built to take advantage of special money-losing 50-year timber sales set up by the Forest Service.

As the Cold War thawed, and the latest boom in Alaska began to fade, the development of oil on the Kenai Peninsula sparked a new surge. Oil seeps had been reported by the Russians in the Cook Inlet area as early as 1853, but not until 1957—with the discovery of a large oil field on the Kenai Peninsula—did Alaska begin to see its future in oil development rather than in gold, fish or timber.

In 1959, Alaska entered the Union as the 49th state. The federal government showered further benefits upon the state, conveying titles to most seaports and airstrips built at federal expense. Perhaps the most important act of largesse granted Alaska title to 104 million acres of land, an area comparable in size to California. This was the largest state land grant in history (most western states received title to approximately five to 10 percent of their total acreages, while Alaska was given 28 percent). And, unlike other western states that received two sections in each township, Alaska was allowed to choose its land from any part of the state. Selections did not have to be finalized until 1984—a deadline later extended to 1994. Alaska also got title to all tidelands and submerged lands within three miles of its coasts. These totaled some 40 million additional acres.

The importance of these land grants became apparent later when the giant Prudhoe Bay oil field was discovered in 1968. The state selected most of the Arctic Coast when oil discoveries seemed imminent and, after the Prudhoe Bay discovery, oil companies paid the state $900 million for oil and gas leases in this area. But this was only the beginning of a windfall oil profit for the state.

The Prudhoe Bay oil field, the largest discovered in North America, contained one quarter of the known petroleum reserves in the United States. Although oil began flowing through the Trans-Alaska Pipeline only in 1977, by 1986 more than half the oil from this giant reserve already had been pumped from the ground.

Oil soon became the lifeblood of Alaska. Some towns are single-industry towns; Alaska is virtually a single-industry state. It is now the second-largest U.S. oil producer after Texas. The Trans-Alaska Pipeline was the largest construction project ever and cost more than $9 billion. By 1982, the petroleum industry generated more than half of Alaska's personal income and employment. Oil royalties made up 80 percent of the state's general revenues during 1984. For example, in 1984, the state collected nearly $2.8 billion in royalties and severance taxes—about $10,000 per resident. This plentiful source of funding allowed Alaska's government to expand significantly. In most states, government employment accounts for 18.7 percent of payrolls, but in Alaska this is doubled—with some 38.8 percent of payrolls, excluding military personnel, derived from government employment. The drop in oil prices during the mid-1980s severely reduced the state's oil revenues and its ability to continue funding projects and services.

Above: Ruins of World War II army camp at Dutch Harbor. TIM THOMPSON

Left: Two or three years before the attack on Pearl Harbor, and before the U.S. military considered the Aleutian Islands tactically important, these Japanese visitors spent a few months in the Aleutians, photographing extensively. Here they pose at Dutch Harbor, which Japanese forces attacked in June 1942 (see page 71). COAST GUARD MUSEUM/NORTHWEST, SEATTLE

Facing page: Fairbanks began as a supply post for local placer mines, but deeper gold deposits that required the use of dredges and other heavy mining equipment allowed the miners to remain in operation longer than those in other gold-producing regions. Unlike many other mining boom-towns, Fairbanks did not disappear, and remains Alaska's second-most-populous city. FRANK NOWELL NEG. 6138, SPECIAL COLLECTIONS, UNIVERSITY OF WASHINGTON

The oil boom and its associated activities prompted a population explosion in Alaska during the 1970s and early 1980s. For example, in 1983, the state's population grew by 10.8 percent. But the dangers of dependence upon a single industry became clear as Alaska's population dropped rapidly, reflecting the decline of oil prices in recent years. Anchorage lost some 20,000 people in 1987 alone, and people joked that the "last one out should turn off the lights and lock the door."

The pipeline and oil development spurred the growth of Alaska's population and prosperity but also contributed to a great sub-division of the Alaskan landscape. When the oil pipeline first was proposed in the late 1960s, most of Alaska was publicly owned and managed by the Bureau of Land Management.

After the oil companies announced that they planned to construct the Trans Alaska Pipeline from Prudhoe Bay to the ice-free port of Valdez, five Native villages near the pipeline corridor filed suit claiming ownership of the pipeline right of way. This crystallized an issue that had simmered for years: exactly what claim did Alaska's Indians, Eskimos and Aleuts have to state lands? The suit threatened to tie up land in litigation for years. Anxious to begin construction of the pipeline without further delay, the oil companies put their considerable political and financial might behind Native claims to resolve the issue quickly

In 1971, Congress passed the Alaska Native Claims Settlement Act (ANCSA), which awarded a cash payment of nearly a billion dollars, and ownership of 44 million acres or

about 12 percent of the state, to Alaskan native people. Acting on the request of Native leaders themselves, ANSCA also established 12 Native regional corporations to manage the money and lands that make Alaska's natives the largest private land owners in the world. For example, Doyon Native Corporation, one of the 12 regional corporations, owns approximately 14 million acres, or about three times the area of New Jersey. In addition to regional corporations, each village also organized as a separate corporation, and obtained title to land near the community.

The Native Corporation selection process entitled the Natives to both surface and sub-surface rights, including full title to oil, gas and other minerals. As a consequence, the corporations have tended to concentrate their land selections on those tracts with high mineral, oil, timber or other known natural-resource potential.

Another offshoot of the Native claims-pipeline debate was the establishment of major new conservation land units in Alaska. A small sub-section of ANCSA, section 17(d)(2), directed the Secretary of Interior to withdraw as much as 80 million acres of public land (an amount later expanded by Congress) for study by the Bureau of Land Management (BLM) as potential new additions to the national park, wildlife refuge and national forest systems. Eventually this study culminated in the Alaska National Interest Lands Conservation Act (ANILCA), passed by Congress and signed into law by President Carter on December 2, 1980, hailed by many as the greatest conservation law in United States history. This sweeping legislation reclassified 104 million acres of Alaska's BLM lands, and includes 43.6 million acres designated as new parks and preserves;

53.8 million acres as new wildlife refuges; and 3.4 million acres as new national monuments on Tongass National Forest lands in southeast Alaska.

Although the creation of new parklands appears to give these lands permanent protection, there was an Achilles' heel in the legislation—a tremendous number of private inholdings within the newly created national parks. For example, 660,000 acres of the 3.6 million acres within the boundaries of Lake Clark National Park and Preserve are privately owned, mostly by Native corporations. This includes three fourths of the park's centerpiece, 50-mile-long Lake Clark. There are more than a million acres of inholdings in the Wrangell-St. Elias National Park. All of these inholdings are potentially open for development and, in some cases, already are being subdivided. In addition, access to many millions of acres of public lands could potentially be controlled or blocked by the strategic location of private tracts in these conservation units. In the long run, probably the only way to ensure full protection of these parklands will be public acquisition of the inholdings.

One pattern dominates Alaska's history. Innumerable booms have been followed by inevitable busts. Furs. Gold. Fish. Military. Now, oil. Remote markets, coupled with the extreme difficulty and expense of development in the state, mean that Alaska's resources must be superlative to have any market value. The world-class Prudhoe Bay oil field, for example, ranks with the largest reserves found in Saudi Arabia and elsewhere. Otherwise, the oil companies could not have afforded development. The average offshore oil well in Louisiana costs $161 per foot to drill, while in Alaska the cost is $385 per foot.

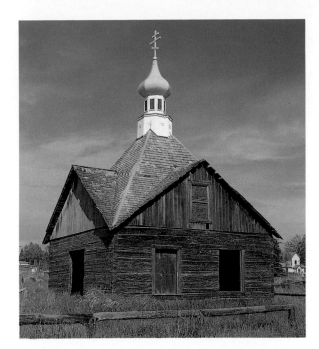

These factors—isolation and high operating costs—influence other areas of the Alaskan economy. Without government subsidies there would be very little timber harvest on national forest lands in Alaska. It is simply cheaper to cut trees in Oregon, Georgia and Maine. As long as there are plenty of trees in those regions, Alaska's resources will remain too expensive for development without being subsidized.

Perhaps Alaska's greatest riches are its magnificent scenery, wildlife resources and wilderness. These match the most spectacular scenery anywhere on the globe. Although they afford less immediate wealth than oil or other exhaustible natural resources, Alaska's national parks, national wildlife refuges, national monuments and wilderness areas will continue to draw people to the state, providing a long-term economic resource, as well as contributing greatly to the quality of life for residents.

Above: *Eskimo stone marker in the hills northeast of Kiana in the Brooks Range. Eskimos erected some of these markers as guide posts, but some merely signalled that a human being had passed this way—that others inhabited this lonely land.* GEORGE WUERTHNER
Left: *An abandoned Russian Orthodox church memorializes early white settlers.* BRUCE SELYEM
Facing page: *The Alaska economy always has ridden a boom-and-bust cycle. The last major boom accompanied the discovery of the Prudhoe Bay oil fields—the largest oil deposit ever found in the U.S. This discovery prompted construction of the Alaska Oil Pipeline and its terminal at Valdez, seen here, the most northerly ice-free port in Alaska.* GEORGE WUERTHNER

RANGES OF THE
SOUTHEAST

Southeast Alaska, about the size of the state of Maine, has unmatched mountain beauty and abundant wildlife. Because of the juxtaposition of sea, mountain forest and glacial ice, the coastline is among the most spectacular in the world. But the magnificent scenery has its costs—flat ground is at a premium, as anyone who has ever flown into the mountain-rimmed Juneau airport can attest. Both Juneau and Ketchikan are built on the sides of mountains, and towns like Skagway occupy narrow valley floors. So rugged is the terrain that no road network connects the major communities, and all travel is by boat or air. Because of the limited transportation system as well as the terrain, some 70 percent of the region's population is concentrated in the urban areas of Juneau, Ketchikan and Sitka.

In this region dominated by mountains and sea, the highest peaks are in the St. Elias Mountains—60 percent of the range lies in Alaska, with the rest in Canada. The highest peak in the Alaska section of the range is 18,008′ Mt. St. Elias, which rises more than three miles above the waters of Yakutat Bay. The St. Elias Mountains are the highest coastal mountains in the world. These lofty mountains consist of several sub-ranges, including the Fairweather and Chilkat ranges, but all are geologically linked. Besides Mt. St. Elias, other high peaks include 15,700′ Mt. Vancouver, 15,300′ Mt. Fairweather, 14,070′ Mt. Augusta, 14,950′ Mt. Hubbard, 13,760′ Mt. Cook and 12,726′ Mt. Crillon.

The St. Elias Mountains are being uplifted as the Yakutat terrane docks onto North America. This 360-mile-long terrane, marked by the northwest-trending Fairweather Fault, is moving at a rate of approximately $2^{1}/_{2}''$ a year.

The numerous earthquakes in this region are attributable to the plate's motions. A number of terranes transported from elsewhere come together in this region. Within Glacier Bay National Park, for example, the Alexander terrane occupies the northern side of the bay, while younger rocks of the Chugach terrane lie on the south side. Mineral concentrations along the margins of terranes within the park create outcrops of zinc, copper, nickel and even gold. These minerals appear among the metamorphosed volcanic and sedimentary rocks, intruded with pockets of granite, that make up the St. Elias Mountains.

The imposing barrier of the St. Elias Range wrings moisture from storms passing inland from the Gulf of Alaska—Yakutat receives 133″ of precipitation annually and the figure is much higher in the mountains. This moisture feeds the largest glaciers in continental North America, including the immense Malaspina Glacier, a 50-mile-wide piedmont glacier larger than the state of Rhode Island. As few as 600 years ago, Yakutat Bay did not exist, but instead was completely filled with glacial ice. Retreat began about 1400 A.D., yet the 92-mile-long Hubbard Glacier at the head of the bay remains as the longest valley glacier in North America.

The mountains that make up Glacier Bay National Park and Preserve include the three-mile-high Fairweather Range to the west and the Chilkat Range to the east. Glacier Bay itself is a relatively recent development. When Captain Vancouver surveyed the Alaskan coast

Facing page; McBride Glacier flows into Muir Inlet in Glacier Bay National Park. LARRY ULRICH

in 1794, he recorded a huge tidewater glacier at the mouth of what is now Glacier Bay. When preservationist John Muir explored the bay in 1879, the glacier had retreated 40 miles forming two arms—Tarr Inlet and Muir Inlet. Now, the glaciers have retreated some 75 miles in all, although a few, like Grand Pacific, have begun to advance once more.

But glacial advances and retreats are not unusual in this region. The last major Ice Age ended 10,000 years ago, when ice buried nearly all of Southeast Alaska. A warming trend about 7,500 years ago melted back the glaciers, and hemlock forests grew in Muir, Adams and other Glacier Bay inlets. Then about 4,000 years ago a change in climatic balance allowed the glaciers to grow again, and these forests were eventually buried by advancing ice sheets. Today, logs and roots from the ancient forests

can be seen where moraines have been washed away exposing these "fossil forests." The wood, perfectly preserved and still burnable, is most of the driftwood one encounters in the upper end of Muir Inlet. As a result of glacial retreat, one massive glacier has melted into 13 tidewater glaciers, each issuing from tributary inlets into the main bay.

The Coast Mountains straddle the British Columbia–Alaska border. They are generally lower than the St. Elias Mountains but still impressive. The highest peaks include 10,023′ Kate's Needle and 9,077′ Devil's Thumb. The Coast Range is made up a variety of metamorphosed sedimentary rock, including slates and schists. Intruded into these slates and schists are granitic rocks—part of the Coast Range granite batholith that extends southward into British Columbia. As a rule, the highest

peaks in the Coast Mountains are made of granite since this rock is the most resistant to erosion:

Glacier Bay is not the only area where glaciers are in retreat. LeConte Glacier, the southernmost tidewater glacier in North America, streams out of the Coast Range near Wrangell. In the last hundred years, it has retreated approximately two and a half miles. Two massive ice sheets—the Stikine and Juneau icefields—cover the crest of the Coast Mountains. The Stikine Icefield stretches for 120 miles and feeds a number of tidewater glaciers, including LeConte, Patterson, Baird, Dawes, North Dawes, South Sawyer and Sawyer. The 30-mile-long Taku Glacier is fed by the Juneau Icefield, as is the Mendenhall Glacier near Juneau.

Paralleling the Coast Mountains for about 300 miles are the islands of the Alexander Archipelago, whose peaks are less than 4,000′ above sea level. Composed of sedimentary and metamorphic rocks, these islands are merely the exposed peaks of a mountain range that has been flooded by rising sea levels since the Ice Age. At one time, massive ice sheets covered all the higher elevations and huge glaciers flowed down channels like Chatham Strait carving out deep valleys that became fiords once the sea level rose. Today, these islands no longer are glaciated, and only a few small cirque glaciers remain along the higher peaks on Chichagof, Kupreanof, Baranof and Admiralty.

Some of the islands of the archipelago are quite large—Prince of Wales Island is the third largest island in the United States after Kodiak and the island of Hawaii—and Admiralty Island is 100 miles long and averages 30 miles wide. The channels separating this maze of islands frequently mark fault lines. For example, Peril

Strait between Baranof Island and Chichagof Island is a major fault. Most of the larger fiords also represent major fault zones. The Lynn Canal and its extension, Chatham Strait, outline a major break in the earth's crust—the west side of the fault is sliding past the east side much as the San Andreas Fault is gradually moving Los Angles closer to San Francisco. The displacement between the two sides of the fault here is 90 miles, making the fault a natural pathway for Ice Age glaciers. The resulting fiord, Lynn Canal-Chatham Strait, is the longest in North America. All these channels and straits form the famed Inside Passage that allows boats relatively tranquil travel away from open Pacific swells.

Since the terrain is so steep and the distance from tidewater to headwaters is relatively short, few rivers in this region are more than 10 to 20 miles long. A number of larger rivers flow out of the interior reaches of the Yukon Territory and British Columbia and breech the barrier of the St. Elias and Coast mountains. These watercourses, such as the Stikine, Taku and Alsek, pre-date the existence of these mountains. As the mountains rose, the streams continued to cut downward through them and maintained their outlets to the sea. At one time the Yukon River also flowed south across the mountains. Even today its headwaters are no more than 33 miles from tidewater near Skagway. But unlike the Stikine or Alsek, the Yukon was not able to cut down fast enough to compensate for mountain uplift. Gradually it changed direction and sought a new outlet to the north; it now makes a 2,000-mile journey to the Bering Sea.

The climate for Southeast Alaska, influenced by the Japanese Current, is mild. Freezing temperatures are infrequent, as is extreme heat, and rainfall is abundant. A sign I once saw at Glacier Bay National Park said: "You can tell when it's summer in Southeast Alaska because the rain is warmer." It definitely rains here, in some places more than an inch a day on the average. There is a precipitation gradient from south to north and west to east. Those mountains lying farthest south and closest to the ocean often receive more 200″ of precipitation annually. Little Port Walter on the southern tip of Baranof Island, for example, receives 221″ of precipitation annually and the mountains above it are showered with 400″ a year! Ketchikan averages 154″ annually, while Juneau receives only 70″. By the time one reaches Skagway, protected from most storms by a ring of mountains, the annual precipitation drops to 26″ —considerably less than New York City's average of 44″.

Above: *Ocean liner dwarfed by peaks in Tarr Inlet, Glacier Bay National Park.* GEORGE WUERTHNER
Facing page: *Skiers climb the Hubbard Glacier below Mount Seattle in the St. Elias Range.* BRIAN OKONEK

Whether a community is on the ocean side or lee side of a mountain mass also influences precipitation. Sitka, facing the open Pacific, records 95″ of precipitation annually, while Angoon, a village on Admiralty Island lying in the rainshadow of the mountains on Baranof Island, receives a mere 40″.

Just as precipitation is generally greater to the south, temperatures are usually lower to the north. Icy blasts from the interior of the Yukon Territory sweep over the Coast Mountains several times a winter, dropping temperatures well below zero in places like Juneau, while Ketchikan—whose record low is minus 4°—is less likely to feel those chilling temperatures.

This climate encourages plant growth and nature has shown little restraint in its extravagance. Walking through the moss-carpeted forest floor is somewhat like walking on a waterbed. Everything—rocks, logs, soil—is covered with a dense growth of vegetation. Sometimes the brush is so thick that hikers can't see what's underfoot, and in front of them is a green wall of leaves. They almost swim through vegetation rather than walk through it. Yet, in spite of this luxuriant growth, timberline is rather low here, compared to the Rockies or other mountain regions of the West. This is due to the cool climate and heavy snow—one does not have to climb very high on a mountain to reach the limit of permanent snow. Timberline is highest in the south—around 3,000′—while in the north it is only 1,800′ due to harsher climatic conditions.

Around Skagway and Haines, influenced by the dry and sometimes cold air that flows across the Coast Mountains from the Yukon, one finds paper birch and the straight Rocky Mountain variety of lodgepole pine, intermixed with more typically coastal species found farther south like mountain hemlock, western hemlock and Sitka spruce. Throughout Southeast Alaska a brushy, short variety of lodgepole pine, often called shore pine, is found scattered in muskeg, where drainage is poor and the water table high.

A number of species reach their northern limits in Southeast Alaska. Western red cedar, a tree common to the west-coast forests in Washington and Oregon, grows no farther north than Frederick Sound. Silver fir barely enters the state near Ketchikan, and subalpine fir is found in a few scattered locations, primarily at timberline along the Alaska-Canada border. Sitka spruce makes up approximately 20 percent of the forest, while western hemlock, a climax forest species highly tolerant of shade, accounts for the lion's share of Southeastern Alaska's trees, making up 70 percent of the forests here.

Rain and mild temperatures also foster wildlife in this region. For example, more bald eagles inhabit Southeast Alaska than anywhere else in the world. Hundred-mile-long Admiralty Island near Juneau is reported to be home to 3,000 of these birds. Eagles as well as many other species in Southeast Alaska depend on the fisheries of more than 1,100 salmon-spawning streams.

Tapping this rich fish resource as well is the region's dense grizzly bear population. In Southeast Alaska, grizzlies occupy only the mainland and the so-called ABC islands of Admiralty, Baranof and Chichagof. Admiralty is thought to have the densest population of grizzly bears on earth—more than one per square mile. Bear trails lace the forests following the major salmon streams and paralleling the bays and inlets. Surprisingly, no black bears are found here, but they are present on all the major islands south of Frederick Sound.

Wolves are also absent from the ABC islands but found south of Frederick Sound. Mountain goats are common on mainland mountains and were introduced to Baranof Island in 1923 and Revillagigedo Island in 1983. Sitka blacktail deer are abundant to the south, but become scarcer to the north. Good swimmers, these deer have been seen crossing channels as wide as 10 miles. Another good swimmer, the moose, has invaded the bottoms of major rivers like the Stikine and recently colonized Glacier Bay, but still is common only around Yakutat. Sea otters once were abundant here but now are limited to a small transplanted population on the west coast of Chichagof Island.

Sea otters first prompted white settlement in Southeast Alaska. Alexander Baranov,

Above: *Russell Island and Tarr Inlet, Glacier Bay National Park.* GEORGE WUERTHNER
Facing page, top: *Port Chilkoot and the Chilkat Mountains.* TIM THOMPSON
Bottom, left: *Sitka spruce forest with moss hangings, Glacier Bay.* GEORGE WUERTHNER
Bottom, right: *Sunset along the west coat of Admiralty Island.* GEORGE WUERTHNER

SCALES AND SUMMIT OF CHILKOOT PASS COPYRIGHT 1898

Above: *The certainty that their fortunes lay beyond led prospectors, with their 2,000 pounds of supplies apiece, over the rigorous Chilkoot Pass in 1898.*
HEGG NEG. 412, MUSEUM OF HISTORY AND INDUSTRY, SEATTLE
Facing page, top left: *Dark streaks of sediment eroded from mountains of the Fairweather Range stripe the Johns Hopkins Glacier, Glacier Bay National Park.* KENT & DONNA DANNEN
Top right: *The first passenger train over the White Pass and Yukon Railway is seen crossing the east fork of the Skagway River in February 1899.* HEGG NEG. 38, MUSEUM OF HISTORY AND INDUSTRY, SEATTLE
Bottom: *Coast Range seen across Endicott Arm.*
GEORGE WUERTHNER

attracted by the rich sea otter hunting grounds, moved the Russian American Fur Company headquarters from Kodiak to Sitka in 1799. Even as the fur trade declined, Sitka remained the center of European influence until 1867, when the United States purchased Alaska.

In 1878, salmon canneries were built at Sitka and Klawock, which signaled the beginning of the next resource boom for Southeast Alaska. Fishing peaked in the 1930s but still accounts for 10 percent of the region's jobs.

Gold was found near Sitka in 1872 and later at Windham Bay in the Coast Mountains south of Juneau. Miners soon spread out across Southeast Alaska looking for new discoveries. Joe Juneau and Richard Harris, two of these prospectors, found a major placer gold deposit on Gold Creek at present-day Juneau in 1880.

Juneau might have gone the way of Windham Bay after the placer deposits were exhausted had it not been for the discovery of hard-rock lode deposits in 1881 on Douglas Island directly across Gastineau Channel from Juneau. This deposit, sold to John Treadwell and known as the Treadwell Mine, eventually employed hundreds of workers, boosting Juneau's population. Juneau then replaced Sitka as the largest town in Alaska—a claim it held until World War II when military growth around Anchorage and Fairbanks allowed those two towns to jump ahead in population.

Skagway also owes its existence to the gold rush days, although no gold was taken here. Its location on Taiya Inlet, at the extreme end of ocean navigation and only 40 miles from the source of the Yukon River over the Chilkoot and White Pass trails, made it a logical staging point for trips to the Klondike and other gold fields of the Interior. Skagway once claimed 10,000 residents. After the gold rush it remained a port and terminus for the White Pass and Yukon Railway, which ceased operation in 1982.

In 1898, more than 30,000 people streamed over the Coast Mountains on the Chilkoot Trail—most of them in winter. Travelers going over the pass met Royal Canadian Mounted Police at the Canadian border atop the pass. All Klondikers were required to have at least 2,000 pounds of supplies before they could legally enter Canada. This required trip after trip up the steep trail, hauling the gear on their backs. Once on the other side, at Lake Bennett—the headwaters for the Yukon River—the '98ers built boats or rafts that they floated 500 miles to Dawson City and the gold fields.

While Skagway's population declined after the gold rush and the town settled into a slow-

FIRST PASSENGER TRAIN OVER WHITE PASS AND YUKON ROUTE TO SUMMIT OF WHITE PASS. FEB. 20=1899.
659   CROSSING EAST FORK OF SKAGUAY RIVER

paced life entertaining visitors during the tourist season, Juneau grew to be the most important town in the region largely due to its position as state capital. But government is a major employer throughout Southeast Alaska, where 38 percent of the people earn their livings as civilian government employees—more than four times the number who work in the timber industry, for example.

The Inland Passage makes traveling Southeast Alaska relatively inexpensive, and tourism is the area's other major economic enterprise. Many Southeast Alaskan ports are stops for either the Alaskan Marine Ferry system or cruise ships. Popular areas for visitors include Misty Fiords National Monument near Ketchikan, historic Sitka, the old gold-rush port of Skagway and Glacier Bay National Park.

TONGASS NATIONAL FOREST

Except for Native Corporation holdings, which amount to 465,000 acres, state holdings amounting to 435,000 acres and the 3.3 million acres in Glacier Bay National Park, nearly all of Southeastern Alaska is part of the sprawling 16.8-million-acre Tongass National Forest—largest in the country. Of these 16.8 million acres, only 9.5 million acres have any forest cover at all. Nearly half of the national forest is alpine or covered with glacial ice. But of the 9.5 million forested acres, only a small portion is considered commercial forestland—primarily those stands located at low elevations in river bottoms and along bays. Of the commercially designated timber, 90 percent is old growth, consisting of trees greater than 150 years in age with some older specimens attaining ages of 800 years!

In the past, foresters referred to this multi-layered old growth as "over-mature" and "decadent." But new research, most of it since 1975, suggests that these "decadent" forests actually form the very center of a complex and interrelated life system that has no duplicate on earth. In fact, the young even-aged stands are biological deserts, while the old-growth forest forms the foundation for a stable and diverse ecosystem. Rotting logs, downed timber and snags are not "wasted" timber, but very essential for proper functioning of the rainforest. Old downed logs, for example, provide long-term nutrient cycling. The large logs that fall into streams make up more than 50 percent of the

fish habitat in small and medium-sized streams. Large old snags make up the bulk of bald eagle nest sites.

Unfortunately, far too much of this magnificent forest is needlessly falling under the assault of the logger's chainsaw. Timber harvest is directed towards the largest, most productive stands, which are also the most important biologically. Hence the impact of timber harvest upon the ecological integrity of the Tongass Forest is disproportionately high. For example, in the snowy Alaskan winter, the umbrella effect of the old growth provides shallow snow areas where Sitka blacktail deer can forage. In clearcuts or young forests, the snow is too deep for the deer to negotiate and they starve. Salmon fisheries also are impacted since timber harvest can change the timing of peak run-off or alter water temperatures. This affects maturity rates for salmon, thus changing downstream migration timing. Sedimentation from roading may bury salmon spawning redds. Loss of large old trees means fewer snags falling into streams to create new fish habitat. These are only a few of the impacts that have been documented. Many other interrelationships remain to be discovered by further scientific study. But we have learned enough to know that the terms decadent and over-mature are entirely misleading descriptions of the extremely rich biological treasures of the old-growth forest.

Despite the presence of large trees, the cost of road construction and worker wages, and the difficulty of logging in this near-vertical mountain world, make timbering the Tongass much more expensive than cutting trees in Lower 48 locations. In order to make timber harvest profitable for timber companies in Alaska, the U.S. taxpayer via the Tongass National Forest subsidizes Alaskan logging operations. A timber company in Alaska can purchase a 100'-tall, 2'-diameter tree for $2.55, while it costs the Forest Service $150 dollars to manage that tree and make it available through timber sales. In what is shaping up as a national scandal, the Tongass National Forest spent approximately $287 million on its timber program between 1982 and 1986, yet collected only $32 million in timber receipts.

To give a specific example, in 1986 the Forest Service planned to build a road up the Lisianski River to access old-growth trees for sale to the Japanese-owned Alaska Pulp Corporation. The cost to the Forest Service was estimated at $4 million, while it was willing to sell the timber for $40,000 to the company. And a salmon run valued at $500,000 a year to commercial fishermen would have been destroyed. At this writing, the sale is under appeal.

Even if the Tongass National Forest's mismanagement is reined in, the Tongass old-growth forests still would be threatened. Alaska's Native Corporations actually cut twice as much timber as the Tongass National Forest. Given their choice of land from nearly any part of the existing Tongass Forest, Native Corporations have chosen the highest-quality timberlands. These bottomlands along estuaries and rivers are far and away the most important wildlife habitats, yet they are being harvested with alarming speed. Since Native timberlands are privately held, they are not even subject to minimal federally-mandated environmental controls (such as sustained-yield forestry), nor are they obliged to protect wildlife habitat or follow other constraints designed to minimize environmental timber-harvest impacts on national forest lands.

Above: *Black Pond, Glacier Bay National Park, was formed when a huge, buried chunk of glacial ice melted.* KENT & DONNA DANNEN
Facing page, top: *A tugboat pulls a log raft past clearcuts on Chichagof Island.* GEORGE WUERTHNER
Bottom: *Pulp mills in Sitka.* CHARLES E. KAY

RANGES OF THE
SOUTH CENTRAL

In a curve from the Yukon border across Prince William Sound to Cook Inlet and the Kenai Peninsula, then south to Kodiak Island, lies Alaska's south-central region. The ranges in this region include the Wrangell, Chugach and Kenai mountains, and mountains on the islands of Prince William Sound and the Kodiak island archipelago.

Mountains hem in all the communities of this region, and some communities such as Valdez and Seward line the fiords. Others, like Anchorage, built on the outwash and moraine left by glaciers at the bases of mountains, have a little more room for growth. Protected from the cold blasts of truly Arctic weather by the Alaska Range, enjoying a climate moderated by the sea's proximity, this region seems to most people the most livable part of the state. Not surprisingly, this region is home to more than two thirds of Alaska's population.

Anchorage, although losing population with the general decline in the Alaskan economy due to the drop of oil prices in the mid-1980s, is still a very large city with well over 220,000 people. But the city is also the workplace for many people living in outlying communities like Palmer and Wasilla. The rest of the region is lightly populated, with Kenai (population 6,200), Homer (3,457), Seward (2,038), Kodiak (13,389), Valdez (3,744) and Cordova (2,223) the largest communities outward from the Anchorage hub.

The most easterly mountains in this region are the Wrangells, part of the 13.2-million-acre Wrangell-St. Elias National Park. The Wrangells are separated from the St. Elias Mountains by the Chitina River and bounded on the northeast by the Copper River Basin. Imagine a mountain the size and shape of

Mount Rainier in Washington, and then picture nearly a dozen of these mountains together in one place and you have a feeling for the spectacular impression the Wrangell Mountains make. Within this mountain block—measuring 100 miles by 60 miles—are some of the highest mountains in the state, with Mt. Bona (16,421'), Mt. Blackburn (16,930') and Mt. Sanford (16,237') all above 16,000' in elevation.

The rocks making up the Wrangells, part of the Wrangellia terrane, arose some 300 million years ago as a volcanic island group near the equator. The islands began to sink and coral atolls (which show up as limestone cliffs today) grew on their tops. Gradually the islands sank even farther, and underwater volcanic eruptions buried the coral. This sequence of rise and fall was repeated several times. Eventually the terrane drifted northward to dock with North America about 120 million years ago. About 10 million years ago volcanos, which we see today as the higher Wrangell peaks including Mt. Drum, Mt. Tanana, Mt. Sanford, Mt. Wrangell and others, began erupting lava over these underlying sedimentary rocks. The massive cone-like shapes characteristic of volcanic peaks are apparent today.

The long, shield-like summit of Mt. Wrangell (14,163') is the youngest of these volcanic mountains and one of the largest andesitic volcanos in the world. It is still active, last erupting in 1930. On the slopes of Mt. Drum three thermal springs, called mud

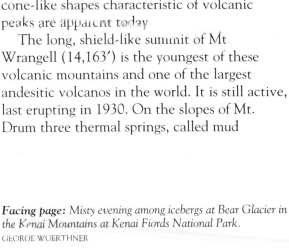

Facing page: Misty evening among icebergs at Bear Glacier in the Kenai Mountains at Kenai Fiords National Park.
GEORGE WUERTHNER

volcanos, indicate that magma is not far below the surface.

Most of the higher peaks in the Wrangells are covered by extensive ice sheets that feed large valley glaciers including the Copper, Sanford, Kuskulana, Kennicott, Chisana and Cheshnina glaciers. The 75-mile-long Nabesna Glacier, longest inland glacier in North America, sweeps off the north slopes of 13,811' Regal Mountain. The run-off from these glaciers carries a tremendous sediment load, and the Copper River—which drains much of the Wrangell Mountains—has one of the highest sediment loads of any Alaskan river.

The cooking process that created this molten volcanic rock concentrated minerals, including gold and copper—both of which have been mined in the Wrangells. On the south side of the Wrangells, near the town of McCarthy, are the Kennicott Copper deposits. The copper was concentrated when underwater eruptions creating the Nikolai basalts overlaid the ancient island group that makes up the Wrangellia terrane. The copper was further concentrated when it migrated as a hypothermal solution upward into the overlying limestone.

Indians of the Copper River Valley used copper implements made from this native copper. The first non-native to record the presence of copper in this region, Lt. Henry Allen, traversed Alaska from the mouth of the Copper River to the Brooks Range in 1885. Allen ventured up the Chitina River as far as Dan Creek, where he met Indians who showed him copper ore that assayed 60 percent pure copper.

Gold miners scouring Alaska near the turn of the century staked claims on the copper and, by 1909, the Kennicott Copper Company was mining ore that was 70 percent pure copper. To move the copper ore from the mines to tidewater for shipment to smelters at Tacoma, Washington, the Copper River and North-western Railway was constructed from Mc-Carthy to Cordova. Passing through the glacier-studded Copper River Canyon, the railroad tracks actually traversed several glaciers, including five and a half miles of the Allen Glacier. Workers continuously relaid track to compensate for glacier movements. The Kennicott Mines closed in 1938 and the old railroad bed now serves as the main road from Chitina to McCarthy.

Lying south of the Wrangell Mountains and curving eastward toward Anchorage and thence south to the Kenai Peninsula are the Chugach Mountains. They have three sections. The eastern Chugach lie to the east of the Copper River, much of them in the Wrangell-St. Elias National Park and Preserve. The central Chugach Mountains lie between the Copper River and the Portage area on Turnagain Arm by Anchorage, and are part of the 5.8-million-acre Chugach National Forest. The third portion is south of Turnagain Arm, one enters the mountainous Kenai Peninsula which, geologically, is merely a southern extension of the Chugach Mountains, although the rugged peaks are called the Kenai Mountains. Much of the Kenai Peninsula is also under some kind of federal management jurisdiction, including

Kenai National Moose Refuge, Kenai Fiords National Park and Chugach National Forest. The entire peninsula is famous for its recreational opportunities, from catching giant king salmon in the Kenai River to kayaking Kachemak Bay, to backpacking on one of the most extensive trail systems in the state. Among the attractions of the Kenai Mountains are beautiful fiord-like glacially-carved lakes including Kenai, Upper Russian, Copper, Ptarmigan, Trail and Crescent lakes. Both Skilak and Tustumena lakes extend out from the mountains, but nevertheless were created by glaciers.

The Chugach Mountains consist of sedimentary shales, siltstones, sandstones, conglomerates and volcanic rocks that have been slightly metamorphosed since their formation some 130 million years ago as part of a volcanic island system somewhere in the Pacific. During the formation of these sedimentary rocks, lush vegetation grew. Later it formed the great coal beds and oil fields found on the Kenai Peninsula and elsewhere in South-Central Alaska. Within this matrix of sedimentary and metamorphic rocks are granitic intrusions and mineralization. The first gold ever discovered in Alaska was found near Cooper Landing by Russians in 1848, but they—afraid that news of it would draw Americans northward—kept the discovery quiet. Later, after America gained ownership, prospectors found gold in 1895 at Hope, Crow Creek and elsewhere. Copper mines in the region included those at Ellamar and Latouche in Prince William Sound.

The Chugach terrane was rafted to Alaska and docked some 65 million years ago. The northern boundary of the range is marked by the Border Ranges Fault, which runs along the

Chitina River westward past Tazlina Lake to the Matanuska Glacier.

South of the Chugach terrane is the Prince William Sound terrane, makes up most of the islands of the same name. The Prince William Sound terrane is composed of a greenish-gray metamorphosed volcanic rock, plus associated sedimentary rocks.

Like the St. Elias Range, the Chugach Mountains are being raised by the collision of the Pacific Plate and the North American Plate, literally giving rise to very high mountains only a few miles from the sea. The highest peak, Mount Marcus Baker, is 13,176'. Other high peaks include Mt. Tom White (11,210'), Mt. Steller (10,617'), Mt. Valhalla (12,135'),

Above: The Copper River in the Wrangell Mountains.
BRUCE SELYEM
Facing page: Matnuska Glacier in the Chugach Mountains.
JEFF GNASS

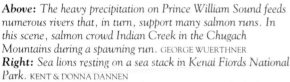

Above: The heavy precipitation on Prince William Sound feeds numerous rivers that, in turn, support many salmon runs. In this scene, salmon crowd Indian Creek in the Chugach Mountains during a spawning run. GEORGE WUERTHNER
Right: Sea lions resting on a sea stack in Kenai Fiords National Park. KENT & DONNA DANNEN
Facing page: Mt. Marcus Baker, at 13,176', is the highest peak in the Chugach Mountains. GEORGE WUERTHNER

Mt. Goode (10,610') and Mt. Witherspoon (12,023'). Only one river, the Copper, actually crosses this mountain barrier.

When moist air masses from the Gulf of Alaska encounter these towering mountains, a tremendous amount of precipitation is wrung from the sky. During the winter of 1952-1953, 974" of snow fell on Thompson Pass in the Chugach Mountains above Valdez! The entire Chugach Mountain complex has been severely glaciated and even today has the greatest concentration of glacial ice in Alaska. Ice sheets drape the highest ridges of the Chugach and Kenai mountains and feed numerous valley glaciers. Bering Glacier, named for Vitus Bering, is the largest glacier in continental

North America, covering some 2,250 square miles; it drains the Bagley Ice Field. The piedmont lobe of the Bering Glacier is 25 miles in diameter, somewhat smaller than the nearby Malaspina Glacier.

Ice sheets cover the mountains near Cordova and feed a number of valley glaciers, including the Childs and Allen glaciers that flow into the Copper River Canyon. Farther west, draped around Mount Witherspoon and Mt. Marcus Baker, huge icefields feed some of the best-known glaciers in the Chugach Mountains: Columbia, Matanuska, Nelchina, Knik and Tazlina. Also dropping from these high peaks are the glaciers found in College Fiord, Barry Arm and Harriman Fiord, which represent the greatest concentration of tidewater glaciers in Prince William Sound.

College Fiord, Columbia Glacier and Harriman Fiord were named by members of the 1899 Harriman Expedition. Funded by E.R. Harriman, owner of the Northern Pacific Railroad, the expedition was the first non-government scientific study of Alaska's natural history and included such notables as preservationist John Muir, William Dall of the Smithsonian Institution (for whom the Dall sheep is named), and geologist Grove Karl Gilbert of the U.S. Geological Survey. The group's photographer was Edward Curtis, who later became famous for his images of American Indians.

The last major ice sheets to the west include the Harding and Sargent icefields, which crown the Kenai Mountains. Harding, named for President Warren Harding, is the largest—some 50 miles by 30 miles across. It feeds the glaciers draining into Kenai Fiords National Park as well as those that feed Tustumena and Skilak lakes on the Kenai lowlands to the west. The slightly smaller Sargent Icefield feeds 25 glaciers, many of them tidewater glaciers emptying into the western edge of Prince William Sound.

At one time, huge glaciers flowed out of the Chugach and Kenai mountains and down Knik Arm and Turnagain Arm to join near present-day Anchorage before emptying into Cook Inlet. As these glaciers retreated, they left behind the till and outwash that Anchorage now is built upon.

The coastline of Prince William Sound, as well as the outer coast of the Kenai Peninsula, is carved by glaciers into deep fiords. Turnagain Arm, south of Anchorage, a fine example of a glacial fiord, separates the Kenai Mountains from the Chugach Mountains. The Chugach Mountains behind Anchorage, as well as the Kenai Mountains south across Turnagain Arm, are defined by a ruler-straight fault that is remarkably evident in satellite photos of the Cook Inlet area.

It was slippage along a fault in Prince William Sound that resulted in the 1964 Earthquake, centered at Miner's Lake. The quake registered 8.6 on the Richter Scale, the largest ever recorded. One hundred thirty-one people died; several communities—such as Valdez, Chenega and Seward—were destroyed. In places the earth was raised as much as 30' and in others it sank 10'. Today along many shorelines, the silver snags of trees indicate where the land sank, allowing salt water to inundate and kill forests. One of the most accessible of these ghost forests lies at Portage, south of Anchorage, near Portage Glacier. The rise and fall of land also affected wildlife. In places, newly-created waterfalls made former salmon-spawning streams impassable. In the Copper River delta, the uplifting disrupted one of the major waterfowl nesting areas in Alaska, since the

now-higher ground provided access for land predators. The world's entire population of dusky Canada geese nests here, and has declined in recent years due to increased predation.

A string of islands south of the Kenai Peninsula, including the Chugach, Barren, Afognak, Shuyak and Trinity islands along with Kodiak, comprises the Kodiak Island Archipelago. They consist of Chugach terrane rocks and are merely a southern extension of this great chain, with the top of a sinking mountain range appearing as the occasional island.

Kodiak, 100 miles by 60 miles, is the largest island in Alaska, with miles of glacially-carved shoreline. More than 40 small glaciers lie in pockets among its highest peaks, which are barely above 4,000' in elevation.

The lack of glaciers means most of the rivers draining the island are clear-flowing, excellent spawning habitat for salmon. The surrounding seas are rich in crab, shrimp and other seafood. As might be expected with such an abundant natural resource, Kodiak is one of the largest fishing ports in the country—second in the United States only to New Bedford, Massachusetts in terms of total value of catch.

The climate of this region is of three varieties—coastal, transitional and continental. Communities like Kodiak lying on the gulf are influenced by the maritime climate. Kodiak averages 57" of precipitation a year and has relatively mild temperatures—its lowest recorded temperature was minus 12°. Yet McCarthy, beyond the coastal Chugach Mountains on the

south slope of the Wrangells, receives only 17″ of precipitation, and has much colder lows, with a minus 58° once recorded there. Anchorage, shielded by the Chugach Mountains from the rainstorms on the gulf but still influenced by the oceanic climate, is transitional between the two and has an annual precipitation of only 15″ and a record low of minus 34°.

The entire coastal region experiences a maritime climate with abundant rainfall and mild, cool weather. The damp, cool climate with heavy snowfall means timberline is very low— in many places at less than a thousand feet on the ocean side of the mountains.

The coastal mountains continue the vegetation patterns of Southeast Alaska, with Sitka spruce and western hemlock dominating. As a rule, though, the trees are not so large as species found in southeastern forests. Mountain hemlock becomes progressively more common as one moves westward to the Kenai Peninsula, and often is the sole representative of the sub-alpine forest zone at timberline. Mountain hemlock also replaces shore pine in muskeg areas in Prince William Sound, where it assumes a shrubby, flat-branched form. Both species of hemlock are absent from Kodiak Island, where the only tree is Sitka spruce. The

spruce only recently gained a toehold on the island's northern tip and gradually is extending its range southward at a rate of one mile per hundred years. Black cottonwood is common along coastal-mountain rivers.

On the interior side of the coastal-mountain barrier, species more typical of a continental climate include white spruce, black spruce, paper birch and aspen. These interior forest species dominate the Wrangell Mountains and the north slope of the Chugach Mountains as well as the rainshadow coastal areas of upper Cook Inlet around Anchorage and on the Kenai Peninsula.

Like the flora, the fauna is a mix of interior and coastal species. The mountains act as a barrier and a climatic filter separating the habitats various animals need. The abundant rainfall ensures numerous rivers and, hence, salmon runs. These fisheries support bald eagles, river otters, minks and, of course, brown and grizzly bears. Kodiak Island is synonymous with bears, and some 2,500 of these intelligent creatures inhabit Kodiak. Biologists believe their ancestors reached the island during the waning days of the Ice Age, when lower ocean levels allowed the bears to walk easily from the mainland. Brown bears are the only bears found on the outer islands of Prince William Sound, including Montague and Hinchinbrook.

The water barrier has prevented many other animals from reaching Kodiak or its sister islands. There are no moose, no Dall sheep or caribou. Both Sitka blacktail deer and mountain goats are found on Kodiak today, but they were introduced as were the elk that roam Afognak Island.

On the mainland, the array of wildlife is broader. As a rule, the mountains facing the ocean support wildlife species similar to those found in Southeast Alaska's Coast Mountains, such as black bears, mountain goats and an occasional moose in major river corridors like the Copper River. Sitka blacktail deer were not native to the region but were introduced to Prince William Sound.

On the inland side of the coastal mountains one encounters species adapted to a drier climate and more typical of Alaska's interior. A small herd of caribou, for example, inhabits the Kenai Peninsula and the Wrangell Mountains. Moose roam the Kenai Peninsula and from Anchorage eastward along the interior side of the Chugach Mountains all the way to the Wrangells.

Dall sheep, intolerant of deep snow, hence confined to the drier rainshadow portions of this region, share the same general range: the inland parts of the Kenai Mountains and throughout the interior portion of the Chugach Mountains, and they are particularly abundant in the Wrangells, where an estimated 20,000 Dall sheep live.

Usually the ranges of mountain goats and Dall sheep do not overlap, but the exception to this rule is found in the Chitina River valley of the Wrangell Mountains, where mountain goats live on the steeper cliffs and sheep on the gentler slopes.

Another introduced mammal, the bison, roams in two herds in the Wrangell Mountains. Bison were common in Alaska at the close of the last Ice Age but died out in the north. The bison now found in various Alaskan herds were introduced from Montana. These animals survive in the drier valleys where the gravel bars of glacial rivers provide some grassland habitat.

Above: Most of Kodiak Island is treeless, covered with a verdant carpet of ferns, grasses and shrubs. CHARLES E. KAY
Left: Rugged peaks feed the Nelchina Glacier on the dry lee side of the Chugach Mountains. GEORGE WUERTHNER
Facing page: Resurrection Bay on the Kenai Peninsula, viewed from Lost Lake Trail. LARRY ULRICH

RANGES OF THE
SOUTHWEST

The mountains of the Aleutian Range begin east of Lake Clark and run south along the spine of the Alaskan Peninsula and thence southwest as the islands of the Aleutian chain. This range marks one of the most active plate margins in Alaska. Here, along a major subduction zone, the Pacific Plate is plowing under the North American Plate, creating the 25,000'-deep Aleutian Trench. The molten rock produced by the friction and melting of the plate margins feeds the 1,400-mile-long chain of volcanos.

Some of the Aleutian volcanos rise more than 32,000' from their bases on the ocean floor. Many still are rising, with Bogoslof emerging from the sea only in the late 1700s. These mountains represent the largest volcanic arc in the United States and, since historical records began in 1760, the majority of Alaska's 70 volcanos has erupted at least once. The March 1986 eruption of Mt. Augustine, in Cook Inlet, was the most recent volcanic eruption in the state.

The Southwest is remote country and as yet has not been adequately surveyed. Some major peaks still lack official heights on topographical maps. Among the more prominent volcanos, from north to south, are 10,016' Iliamna, 10,197' Redoubt, 6,771' Four Peaked Mountain, Kukak Volcano, 7,090' Snowy Mountain, 6,715' Mt. Katmai, Aniakchak Crater, 8,225' Mt. Veniaminof, 7,028' Pavlof Sister and Pavlof Volcano. The Aleutian Islands themselves are nothing more than a volcanic mountain range, with the highest peak being 9,372' Shishaldin Volcano on Unimak Island.

The rocks from these recent volcanic eruptive centers cover older sedimentary rocks of marine shales, siltstones and sandstones that make up the Peninsular terrane. In places granitic batholith rocks are exposed, indicating old centers of volcanic activity and solidified volcanic breccia, a mixture of volcanic rocks and bombs, is apparent along lakes Iliamna and Grosvenor as well as elsewhere in the region. Volcanic bombs, so full of air bubbles that they float, were blown out with the eruption of Mt. Katmai in 1912 and now commonly bob in the waters of Naknek Lake.

Nowhere is the mountain barrier more than 40 miles wide. Along most of its western flank, at least on the Alaskan Peninsula, it borders by a relatively flat outwash plain. Underlying this marshy plain and in the shadow of Bristol Bay are oil deposits that one day may be tapped.

The most famous of Alaska's volcanic eruptions occurred in June of 1912 within what is now Katmai National Park and Preserve. Some 33 million tons of rock exploded from the earth in two and half days, throwing seven cubic miles of ash and dust 25 miles into the upper atmosphere—enough to darken and cool the entire Northern Hemisphere 1.8°. The explosion was heard 900 miles away in Ketchikan. Across the Shelikof Strait, Kodiak was the major community nearest the blast zone. Immediately following the eruption, ash was so thick that lighted lanterns were invisible at arm's length, even though this was the height of the summer daylight season. Lightning, almost unheard-of in this region, accompanied the ashfall that totaled 11″ to 16″.

Facing page: The Gulf of Alaska and Mt. Douglas on the Aleutian Chain. KENNAN WARD

Three years later, and again in 1916 and 1917, the botanist Robert Griggs led National Geographic Society expeditions to the Katmai region to view the destruction. After climbing Mt. Katmai and finding a small blue lake in the caldera, Griggs passed into what is now known as the Valley of Ten Thousand Smokes. Griggs described the sight: "The whole valley as far as the eye could reach was full of hundreds, no thousands—literally tens of thousands—of smokes curling up from its fissured floor. It was as though all the stream engines in the world, assembled together, had popped their safety valves at once and were letting off surplus steam in concert." All vegetation was incinerated, and the explorers could use the steam coming from the fumaroles to cook with—steam six inches down one hole registered 212°.

Geologists believe a super-heated cloud of ash and gas swept down the valley for 17 miles,

incinerating every living thing in its path. The hot ash continued to turn trapped water into steam for years afterward, but eventually this ash layer cooled and there no longer are any steam vents in the valley. Although the ash is now cool, little vegetation has been able to establish itself on the droughty ash soils. The valley still has an other-worldly appearance, so much so that astronauts trained here prior to moon walks.

Geologists now speculate that the top of Mt. Katmai collapsed as a result of parasitism by another nearby crater—Novarupta, which drained magma away from Katmai, causing the mountain to collapse into itself in much the same way as Crater Lake caldera in Oregon formed. And, as with Crater Lake, there is now a 700′-deep blue lake in the center of the Katmai caldera. Several other volcanos in the Katmai region have erupted since the massive

1912 event, and no one would be surprised if mounts Griggs, Martin, Mageik or Trident erupted today.

At the time of the 1912 eruption, glaciers covered Mt. Katmai's flanks. The heat during the eruption melted those glaciers, but today new glaciers cloak Katmai's flanks. This is one of the few places in the world where the exact age of a glacier is known.

The entire area was set aside as a national monument in 1918, and since has been enlarged and made into a 3.9-million-acre national park and preserve. Just south of Katmai is another volcanic crater preserved as a national monument—Aniakchak Crater. Aniakchak erupted in 1931 and the six-mile-diameter caldera is one of the largest in the world. Inside are cinder cones, hot springs and Surprise Lake, fed by hot springs, which never freezes over.

Glaciers still cover most of the highest peaks in the Aleutian Range, and evidence of past glaciation is everywhere. Much of the east coast of the Alaskan Peninsula is studded with fiords and several glaciers descend to within a few miles of the sea even today.

One of the other special features of the Alaskan Peninsula is the abundance of large lakes. Most of them were glacially carved and then dammed by moraine as a glacier retreated. Here are some of Alaska's most beautiful bodies of water: 50-mile-long Lake Clark, Twin Lakes, Telaquana Lake, Tazmina Lake and Kontra-shibuna Lake. Other lakes such as Naknek Lake are more sprawling, edging out from the mountains into the coastal plain beyond. The glacial origins of Iliuk Arm on Naknek Lake are detectable in the terminal moraine near Brooks Camp, which nearly cuts the arm off from the rest of the lake. Other large lakes that owe their origins in part to glaciers are Iliamna, Becharof, Ugashik, Nonvianuk and Coville. Many of the rivers that feed these lakes still originate in glaciers. The lakes act as giant settling ponds, so that by the time water leaves one of them, it runs clear.

Freedom from the weight of glacial ice has caused much of the area to begin a rebound process called isostatic adjustment. The north shore of Lake Iliamna, the last portion of the lake basin to be deglaciated, is rising faster than its south shore, causing the lake bed to tilt southward. The rebounding also may be causing the Kvichak River, Iliamna's outlet, to migrate southward.

Commercial, subsistence and sport fishermen all can thank the glaciers for Bristol Bay's reputation as the trophy fishing region of the state. The key element is the presence of lakes connected to the sea by short rivers, which form ideal habitat for cold water species like rainbow trout, sockeye salmon, silver salmon and others. Sockeye salmon in particular depend upon the lakes, since they must spend one to two years in a freshwater lake before moving to the sea.

Earthquakes are common, but because of the remoteness of the region, most pass without notice in the outside world. Occasionally, seismic sea waves set up by Aleutian earthquakes do grab the world's attention, as occurred in 1946 when an earthquake of 7.4 on the Richter scale sent a 100' wave outward. It destroyed the Scotch Cap lighthouse in the Aleutians and raced at more than 500 miles per hour to Hawaii, where it swept ashore killing 159 people.

As a result of plate convergence, the region is being uplifted at a rate of one to two feet per century along faults. At Kamishak Bay and on Augustine Island, former shorelines are clearly visible 50' to 90' above the present ocean level.

Above: Looking down into Mt. Katmai caldera, Katmai National Monument.
Left: The desolation of the ash flow still is evident in the Valley of Ten Thousand Smokes nearly 80 years after the explosion of Mt. Katmai in 1912. Cloudy weather is common to the region.
Facing page: Among the still-rising volcanos of the Aleutian Islands. TIM THOMPSON PHOTOS

Above: Glacially-carved 50-mile-long Lake Clark, cradled by the Chigmit Mountains, is the centerpiece for Lake Clark National Park.
Facing page: An icy mantle of glaciers hides the fires inside 10,197′ Mt. Redoubt, one of more than 70 active volcanos in Alaska. Volcanos like this dominate the spine of the Alaska Peninsula and continue throughout the Aleutian Islands. This line of volcanos marks the collision of two major crustal plates as the Pacific Plate is subducted beneath the North American Plate. GEORGE WUERTHNER PHOTOS

One of the major faults, the Bruin Bay Fault, shows sideward displacement of as much as 40 miles over its 300-mile length between Mt. Susitna by Anchorage and Becharof Lake. The linear valley occupied by Lake Clark marks another major fault, while the Tlikakila and Chokotonk rivers in the upper end of Lake Clark both follow branches of this same fault.

Besides having a reputation for earth movements, this region lies between two of the stormiest bodies of water in the world—the Bering Sea and the Gulf of Alaska. The collision of the warm Japanese Current with the cool currents coming south from the Arctic

Ocean produces extremely foul weather. Measurable precipitation occurs on more than 200 days of the year and, on some islands in the Aleutians, there are only an average of 30 clear days a year! Adak, for example, receives precipitation 261 days a year (averaging a total of 62″), with fog for 158 days. Yet the coldest temperature ever recorded here was 3°. The region has one of the mildest climates in Alaska, although the farther north one goes, particularly north of Iliamna Lake, the more the climate resembles that of Alaska's.

For example, Port Alsworth on Lake Clark, although no more than 30 air miles from the ocean, receives only 17″ of precipitation a year, while locations on the Cook Inlet side of the coast may get 40″ to 80″. It has reached 55° below zero here, while temperatures below zero are a rarity farther south in the Aleutian chain. But the amount of clear weather does not seem to be much greater than farther south. Iliamna averages 216 cloudy days, 68 partly cloudy days and 81 days with clear skies each year—most of the last in winter. The rainiest months are August and September.

The cool, cloudy weather is responsible for the lack of tree cover over most of the Alaskan Peninsula and in the Aleutians. Species typical of the Interior forests of Alaska dominate the area west of the mountains around Lake Clark south to Katmai. Here grow white spruce, black spruce, balsam poplar and paper birch. Alders cover nearly all slopes, particularly between timberline and the alpine tundra zone. On the coast, Sitka spruce is found along Cook Inlet as far south as Kamishak Bay, but just a little south of this region it is too cloudy, cool and windy for tree growth. The Aleutians have the lowest level of solar radiation in North America and it is difficult for trees to reproduce seeds under such conditions. In a few locations, Russians, Americans and others have planted conifers and a few survive, but otherwise the Aleutians and the lower half of the Alaskan Peninsula are among the most extensive treeless zones in the world. Shrubs like alder and willow dominate protected sites, while moist tundra characterizes the lowlands, particularly along the western edge of the Alaskan Peninsula. Alpine tundra dominates the rest of the land. In summer, the vegetation of heath, grasses and sedges is surprisingly lush, covering the islands in an emerald cloak.

The wet weather doesn't seem to bother the wildlife for which this region is renowned. Most of the peninsula and islands boast national wildlife refuge or national park designation. Lands protected on the Alaskan Peninsula include, from north to south, Lake Clark Park and Preserve, Katmai Park and Preserve, Becharof Lake Wildlife Refuge, Alaskan Peninsula Wildlife Refuge, Aniakchak Crater Monument and Izembek Wildlife Refuge. Nearly the entire Aleutian chain is part of the Aleutian Islands National Wildlife Refuge.

Wildlife varies and species change from the Cook Inlet region southward. The Chigmit Mountains around Lake Clark mark the southern limits for Dall sheep, a species that requires arid conditions with limited snow cover—something progressively scarcer farther down the peninsula. Moose inhabit the entire peninsula, although they were apparently rare here prior to the late 1800s. Unimak Island, the first island south of the Alaskan Peninsula, marks the natural limit for caribou, grizzly bear, wolf, wolverine, ground squirrel, weasel and porcupine. Almost all the mammals now found on the Aleutians beyond Unimak were introduced by humans.

Caribou were transplanted to Adak and today number in the thousands, while reindeer roam Umnak and Atka islands. Imported horses, cattle, sheep and even bison form wild herds. There are no frogs, amphibians or reptiles here, although the mild temperatures might be favorable. One problem is a lack of insect life—high winds make life difficult for flying insects, including mosquitoes.

The mountains of the Aleutian Archipelago and Alaskan Peninsula are probably Alaska's least-known. Once an estimated 25,000 Aleuts lived in the Aleutian Islands, and Eskimos inhabited the upper portion of the Alaskan Peninsula from Port Moller northward along Bristol Bay. Indian people reached into the northernmost part of the region by Lake Clark. Except for a few villages on the larger lakes like Iliamna and Clark, most of the native people lived on the coast. These coastal people considered the interior highlands dangerous, for there dwelt the "Outside Men" who sought to lure men into the mountains to meet their deaths. Except for a few specific trade routes that crossed the Alaska Peninsula—one went past Mt. Katmai and down to Naknek Lake and another crossed from Cook Inlet to Pedro Bay on Iliamna Lake—most of this region, even then, was untouched wilderness.

Natives of the region lived in subterranean sod huts dug into hillsides, in small permanent villages usually with no more than 60 people, although a few had 200 to 300 people. Most villages were built on promontories where they could be defended easily. Warfare between groups was common since personal prestige was acquired in battle. Another main purpose of war was to acquire slaves. Slaves did much of the

drudgery and could be sold or killed at whim, both of which displayed the owner's wealth and conferred great status on him.

By 1745, just four years after Vitus Bering put Alaska on European maps, Russian fur traders were exploring the chain, eventually reaching Kodiak Island and Southeast Alaska. Not all the Russian dealings with the Aleuts were pleasant. The Russians enslaved some hunters and forced them to hunt sea otters. Other Aleuts traded freely with the Russians, but hostilities increased until 1763, when Aleut warriors attacked several Russian hunting camps, killing more than 200 men. Ivan Korovin, seeking revenge, led a party of fellow survivors that attacked a number of Aleut villages, killing hundreds and breaking spears, kayak-like Aleut baidarkas and other tools needed for survival. This successfully broke the resistance of the Aleuts.

The Russian government was outraged by Korovin's behavior and instituted a judicial review. He was recalled to Russia, where he died destitute. After this episode, the Russian government mandated a policy of fair treatment of Aleuts and outlawed the practice of taking natives hostage to ensure cooperation. But old ways die slowly far from the seat of power, so traders did not always adhere to these laws. Nevertheless, over time, some Russians forged a more harmonious relationship, paying wages to hunters and living essentially like Aleuts themselves, even taking Aleut wives. Today nearly all Aleuts are of mixed blood and Russian last names are common.

Although the Russians instituted conservation measures to preserve fur numbers, they were not the only Europeans dealing in the fur trade. The British, Americans and others also traded with natives for the pelts of sea otter and fur seal and as a result the animal populations fell. Conservation measures were totally ignored once the Americans took over Alaska in 1867 and the fur harvest in the first 23 years of American control exceeded the total harvest during the past 125 years of Russian domination. By 1910, just one year before all hunting of sea otters was outlawed, a hunting crew with 12 baidarkas captured only 14 pelts in an entire summer of hunting! As the fur trade declined, so did interest in the Aleutians.

After wild fur-bearing animals had been decimated, some trappers stocked islands with foxes. These animals breed prolifically and, for a while, fox farming was big business.

In addition to the fur trade, fisheries gained an important foothold in the region when canneries were built in Bristol Bay during the late 1800s. By 1897, canneries were operating on the Kvichak, Ugashik and Naknek rivers. But few people went inland, and Lake Clark was not discovered until the winter of 1890-1891, when writer Alfred Schanz and trader John Clark journeyed up the Nushagak River and portaged to the lake that now bears Clark's name. After the Klondike gold rush put Alaska on the map, the U.S. Geological Survey conducted some investigations of the area, but even these were mostly coastal surveys.

The Aleutians and the Alaskan Peninsula remained a region known only on its coast. Except for the Bristol Bay fisheries, it remained outside the interest of most Alaskans as well as other Americans until World War II, when the Aleutians became a contested battleground for control of the Pacific flyways.

The Japanese strategy in the Aleutians was designed to divert American attention and military strength from the South Pacific. Capture of a position in the Aleutians would have put the Japanese within a 12-hour flight of such strategic targets as the Boeing airplane plant in Seattle and the Bremerton, Washington, navy yard.

On June 2, 1942, the Japanese launched an air attack on Dutch Harbor on Unalaska Island in the Aleutians. American forces successfully defended the island, but several days later Japanese land forces invaded Attu and Kiska islands. On May 11, 1943, American troops landed at Attu. The battle was waged for several weeks. Cut off from supply ships, Japanese Colonel Yasuyo Yamasaki decided to make one last banzai attack. All the wounded in his hospital were killed and the able-bodied prepared for the attack. On May 29, Yamasaki led the charge and nearly overran the American position. But in the end the attack failed and the Japanese soldiers, rather than suffer the disgrace of surrender, committed suicide. Only 28 Japanese were captured alive and an estimated 2,351 died, many by their own hands.

The American forces suffered heavily also. There were 3,829 casualties—in terms of the proportion of troops involved, the attack on Attu was the second costliest American battle in the Pacific after Iwo Jima. Later that summer, American forces invaded Kiska Island only to find that 5,000 Japanese soldiers had slipped away in the fog. American soldiers, nervous after the attack on Attu, shot at each other, killing 25 and wounding 31 others.

Today the military is still the major employer in the region and the naval base at Adak is the largest settlement in the island chain. Dutch Harbor seems to fluctuate as a commercial fishing port, at times being the major crab producer in the country. In the Iliamna and Lake Clark area, trophy fishing has become a major source of tourist dollars, where fancy lodges charge visitors $3,000 a week to fish for rainbow trout, lake trout and salmon. But most of this region is still more a home for wildlife and wild winds than for humans and, given its remote location, it's likely to stay that way for years to come.

Above: The Meshik River and Peninsula Range on the Alaska Peninsula near Port Heiden.
Facing page: Two fishermen stand tense and ready to launch their canoe as a brown bear approaches them near the mouth of the Brooks River at Katmai National Park. Brown bears thrive in the mountains of the Alaska Peninsula, with their rich salmon runs. GEORGE WUERTHNER PHOTOS

ALASKA RANGE

While most people outside Alaska would be hard-pressed to recognize the names of Mt. St. Elias or Mt. Marcus Baker or even the Arrigetch Peaks, they have heard of Mt. McKinley. It has name recognition—and for good reason: it is the highest peak in North America. At 20,320', McKinley dominates the skyline over much of Alaska.

McKinley is the high point of one of Alaska's most spectacular mountain uplifts—the Alaska Range. Inland, but more or less paralleling the coastal mountains, the Alaska Range is marked by the 600-mile Denali Fault System—longest fault in North America—and can be divided into a number of sub-ranges with different names. Geologically, the range begins with the Kluane Range of the Yukon Territory. It passes into Alaska as the Nutzotin Mountains, then Mentasta Mountains, and into what is sometimes referred to as the Eastern Alaska Range, which includes the Mt. Kimball area between the Glenn and Richardson highways and the Mt. Hayes peak complex between the Richardson and Parks highways. The portion west of the Parks Highway, including most of Denali National Park and Preserve and marked by Mt. McKinley, is known as the McKinley sub-range. The last segment of the Alaska Range swings southward directly across Cook Inlet from Anchorage. This includes the Revelation and Tordrillo mountains. Although the Talkeetna Mountains are not a part of the Alaska Range, they are discussed in this chapter since they lie sandwiched between the Chugach Mountains and the Alaska Range northwest of Palmer.

Despite the occasional high peak like McKinley, overall the Alaska Range averages only between 6,000' and 9,000' in elevation.

The range, particularly in the Mt. McKinley region, is being pushed up by the Pacific Plate presently being subducted under the edge of the North American Plate all along the gulf coast.

A number of high peaks punctuate the Alaska Range, separated by intervening mountains of nearly average height. In the east among the Nutzotin Mountains are a few unnamed peaks 8,500' or slightly higher. In the Mentasta Range to the north and west Mt. Noyes (8,235') is the highest. Beyond Mentasta Pass, Mt. Kimball at 10,300' is the dominant mountain. Beyond Kimball and west of the Delta River a group of dramatic, high, glaciated mountains includes Mt. Hayes (13,700'), Mt. Hess (12,030'), Mt. Deborah (12,540') and Mt. Moffit (13,020'). After McKinley and a few of its neighboring peaks, these are the highest mountains in the Alaska Range.

Despite the spectacular presence of Hayes, Hess, Deborah and Moffit, McKinley still remains the undisputed "king" of Alaska mountains. It's one of the most massive mountains in the world and has two summits—a north peak (19,470') and a south peak (20,320'). Other high peaks crowd around McKinley, including 17,395' Mt. Foraker, 14,580' Mt. Hunter, 13,170' Mt. Silverthrone, 14,530' Browne Tower and 12,052' Mt. Mather. Any of these peaks, if it were in isolation, would of itself be considered a large Alaskan mountain, but next to McKinley they lose much of their dramatic impact.

The western portion of the Alaska Range curves southward from Rainy Pass and crashes

Facing page: Caribou bulls and Mt. McKinley, the highest mountain in North America, which dominates the central portion of the 600-mile-long Alaska Range. RICK McINTYRE

Above: The east fork of the Toklat River and Polychrome Glacier viewed from Polychrome Mountain, Denali National park. JEFF GNASS
Right: Looking southwest from Igloo Mountain to the Wonder Lake road in Denali National Park. RON SPOMER
Facing page: As much as possible, the buildings of Independence Mine State Historic Park are being stabilized. This hard-rock gold mine in the Talkeetna Mountains once employed 200 men. KENT & DONNA DANNEN

into the Aleutian Range on the west side of Cook Inlet across from Anchorage. The highest mountains in this area are found in the volcanic peaks of the Tordrillo Mountains which include Mt. Spurr (11,070′), Mt. Gerdine (11,258′) and Mt. Torbert (11,413′).

Lying just south of the Alaska Range and to the east of the Parks Highway are the Talkeetna Mountains. The Talkeetnas are not excessively high—the highest peaks located at the headwaters of the Sheep River and Talkeetna River near Sovereign Mountain are less than 9,000′—yet the glaciated, granitic peaks of these mountains are quite impressive to anyone who has taken the time to travel up into them. They remain among Alaska's undiscovered ranges even though they are no more than an hour-and-a-half drive from Anchorage.

The Talkeetna Mountains are the most northerly extension of the Peninsula terrace that makes up the rocks found on the Alaskan Peninsula. They were volcanic islands that were rafted to their present position millions of years ago. Subsequently they eroded down to the intrusive granitic bodies that mark the roots of ancient volcanos.

Like the Talkeetna Mountains, the rocks making up the Alaska Range are a composite collection of terranes formed elsewhere and later plastered onto the growing continental margin. Part of the Alaska Range is made of segments of the Wrangellia terrane, originally formed as volcanic islands near the equator. As the islands sank, coral atolls formed around them so that today these rocks are primarily eroded volcanic breccias flows overlaid by limestone.

The McKinley terrane, which includes Mt. McKinley, is composed from the eroded remains of another volcanic island chain. The sedimentary rocks include shales, mudstones and sandstones, and in places these sediments were metamorphosed. As with all volcanos, some of the magma did not reach the earth's surface, but cooled in place deep in the ground. This led to the formation of granite bodies that today formed as some of the most dramatic peaks and valleys of the Alaska Range, such as Ruth Gorge, Mt. McKinley, Moose Tooth, Mt. Foraker, Mt. Hunter and the Cathedral Spires.

All of the Alaska Range once was glaciated and bears the marks of glacial erosion. Today, we are in a period of glacial retreat and re-trenchment. That fact, combined with relatively low elevation of the Mentasta and Nutzotin mountains and their position in the rainshadow of the high Wrangell and St. Elias mountains, leaves the Alaska Range with little glacial cover. Nevertheless, the rest of the Alaska Range to the west, both higher and exposed directly to moisture-bearing air masses from the Gulf of Alaska via Cook Inlet, is characterized by massive icefields with well developed valley glaciers radiating from their flanks.

Most of the glaciers in the eastern Alaska Range are retreating. But the 25-mile-long Black Rapids Glacier, visible across the Delta River from the Richardson Highway, has interrupted its retreat with several advances, including a spectacular three-mile surge during the winter of 1936-1937. During its maximum advance, the Black Rapids Glacier was moving at a rate of more than 100' a day!

The largest glaciers exist near the highest peaks in and around the McKinley massif. Because precipitation is greater on the south side of the range, glaciers on this side are typically longer and thicker than those on the north side. Radiating out from McKinley like spokes from a wheel are the longest Alaska

Range glaciers—Kahiltna (43 miles), Muldrow (40 miles) and Ruth (36 miles).

The Muldrow Glacier is perhaps the best known of these McKinley glaciers since its moraine-covered terminus is within sight of the Eielson Visitor Center in Denali National Park and Preserve. In the days before airplane access to the mountain, climbers used to cross the McKinley River and then hike up the Muldrow Glacier to Karstens Ridge, thence to the summit. Although the Muldrow Glacier is usually quiet and is at present slowly retreating, during the spring of 1956 and continuing through the following year, the Muldrow Glacier experienced a surge that pushed it down the valley at a rate of 10" per minute or 1,150' per day!

The last major glacial area is in the Tordrillo and Revelation mountains at the southwest end

of the Alaska Range. Situated on Cook Inlet close to the maritime Gulf of Alaska climate, these peaks sport extensive glaciers considering their modest heights. Some of the longer ice rivers reach lengths of 15 to 25 miles. Lakes are relatively scarce in the Alaska Range. The few large lakes that do exist are found here on the edge of the Tordrillo Mountains, including Beluga Lake and the spectacular 15-mile-long Chakachamna Lake that separates the Tordrillo Mountains from the Chigmit Mountains.

Other Ice Age influences are evident throughout the Alaska Range. Mentasta Pass near Tok was once a spillway for a large glacial lake, Lake Atna. The lake formed when glacial ice blocked the Copper River and water filled the entire Copper River Basin. The landscape around Glennallen is rolling-to-level because it is the old lake bed.

Above: Looking south from the Alaska Range to the Talkeetna Mountains near Broad Pass.

Facing page, top: *Mts. Deborah, Hess and Moffit represent the highest peaks in the Alaska Range outside the Mt. McKinley region. In this view of a tundra pond on the south side of the range, Mt. Deborah is visible at the extreme right.*

Bottom: *Alaska Range in Denali National Park. Glaciers feed the Toklat River, giving it a muddy appearance.*

GEORGE WUERTHNER PHOTOS

The climate of the Alaska Range is influenced by its position in relation to the ocean and other mountain ranges. For example, the Tordrillo Mountains lie close to the ocean and receive more annual precipitation than, say, the Nutzotin Mountains lying in the rain shadow of the Wrangells and St. Elias Range. As a rule the south side of the range receives far more precipitation than does the north side. This is reflected in the vegetation. The south side has a far larger shrub zone, while the north side has extensive dry tundra uplands. The north side, facing the Yukon drainage basin, is

very cold, while the south slope tends to have a more moderate climate due to the proximity of the ocean. Nevertheless, the Alaska Range as a whole has a continental climate—warm summers and cold winters. Weather records from Denali National Park indicate annual precipitation is only 15″, most of it coming in summer. The frequent rainy weather during the summer tourist season often obscures Mt. McKinley and a visitors frequently ask, "Is the mountain out today?" Most of the time the answer is no, since McKinley is visible only some 35 percent of the time.

Despite its height, McKinley is not a particularly difficult mountain to climb. In fact, in 1987, 817 climbers attempted the summit, although only 251 people succeeded. Technical aspects of climbing McKinley do not deter people, the weather does. In combination with the extreme cloudiness, temperatures can be very low—even in summer. In winter, they are absolutely frigid: a temperature of 95° below zero was registered on a minimum-recording thermometer left at 14,500′ by an expedition! This kind of temperature, combined with winds of 150 miles per hour and the great height of McKinley, makes any attempt on its summit more than a mere summer outing.

One of the first climbers to attempt the arctic peak was Dr. Frederick Cook. Cook, a tested polar explorer, first attempted a climb in 1903, and made it to about 11,000′ before turning back. Cook was a determined man and returned in June of 1906. He again failed to reach the summit. Then, later that summer, Cook journeyed from Cook Inlet to the Alaska Range, and returned in 12 days claiming he had reached the summit. His claims were disputed from the start, and a number of parties followed, all attempting to disprove Cook's claims.

Then in 1909, a group of miners were sitting around Fairbanks during the winter discussing Cook's claims—some believing the veteran arctic explorer and others discrediting him. Finally, those who doubted Cook's claims decided to climb the mountain themselves to prove once and for all the truth of the matter, or so the story goes. In any event, bets were placed and, in late December, four sour-doughs—Thomas Lloyd, Charles McGonagall, Billy Taylor and Pete Anderson—mushed from Fairbanks bound for McKinley. The members of the Sourdough Expedition had no previous climbing experience, nor did they have any special equipment. Eating bacon and beans, using dog sleds to carry most of their load up the mountain, the group eventually worked their way up the Muldrow Glacier to a base camp at 11,000'. From there, three of them launched a summit assault armed with a thermos of hot chocolate and a bag of doughnuts. Two made the North Peak (which from Fairbanks looks like the higher mountain) where they planted a 14' spruce flagpole. They then made a hasty retreat, returning to camp with two doughnuts to spare!

The sourdoughs' claim that they reached the summit in one day was difficult to believe, and no one could see the flagpole they supposedly left on the summit. New efforts were made to climb the mountain.

In 1913, the Episcopal Archdeacon of the Yukon, Hudson Struck, along with Harry Karstens (Karstens Ridge on McKinley is named for him), Robert Tatum and Walter Harper were on the mountain trying to reach the summit. At 15,000', one member of the party spied a flagpole near the slightly lower north summit, which vindicated the claims of the sourdoughs. Unfortunately for the sourdoughs,

the North Peak is slightly lower than the South Peak, and the honor of being the first successful climbers on McKinley went to the Struck expedition.

Although McKinley dominates Denali National Park and Preserve, it was wildlife, not the mountain, that led to the area's establishment as a park. In fact, until the park was expanded by the Alaska National Interest Lands Conservation Act in 1980, only half the mountain, the north side, was officially in the park.

The park idea had its beginnings with a big-game hunter, Charles Sheldon. Sheldon, independently wealthy, loved to study wildlife and was a passionate hunter. In 1906, Sheldon, along with guide Harry Karstens (who would become the first superintendent of Mt. McKinley National Park) spent a summer hunting sheep and observing the wildlife on the

north slope of the range within what is now the park. Sheldon found the north slope of the Alaska Range to be a wildlife paradise filled with caribou, Dall sheep, moose and grizzly bears. So enchanted was Sheldon by the wild country and its diversity of wildlife resources that he came back the following summer, and stayed all winter so he could more fully appreciate the region's wildlife resources. Sheldon built a cabin on the Toklat River and explored the surrounding countryside by dog sled, making notes, "collecting" a few specimens and enjoying the wild beauty of this rugged land.

At the same time that Sheldon was conducting his wildlife studies, gold was discovered on Glacier Creek in the Kantishna Hills just north of McKinley. The population of miners reached

its height during the years Sheldon was in the region. Market hunters regularly combed the hills seeking out wild game for meat. Sheldon believed that this unregulated hunting—with no bag limits, seasons or other conservation limits—was certain to wipe out the region's wildlife. Thus, to protect the wildlife, he proposed establishing a national park centered on North America's highest peak. He promoted the idea with lectures, letters and lobbying of influential friends and members of Congress. Sheldon even convinced the Boone and Crockett Club, a hunting group to which he belonged, to promote the park idea. In 1917, President Wilson signed a bill creating Mt. McKinley National Park. The original park boundaries have been expanded several times,

most recently in 1980 when the park was enlarged to 6 million acres.

Today Denali National Park and Preserve is the single greatest tourist attraction in Alaska. Originally, access to it was via the Alaska Railroad, which stopped at the entrance. When the George Parks Highway between Fairbanks and Anchorage was completed in 1972, visitation doubled to 88,000 from the figure recorded during the previous year. By 1984, the numbers had risen to 394,000 people.

Although Denali is still relatively wild due to legislative protection, the Tordrillo Mountains area of the Alaska Range is wild because these mountains are difficult to reach despite their relative proximity to Anchorage. But the Tordrillos may not remain isolated much longer. A host of resource developments are occurring in the coastal plain east of the Tordrillos, including timber harvest, oil, gas, and coal development. Coal is particularly abundant in several regions of the Alaska Range, but the Beluga coal field just east of the Tordrillo Mountains is one of the higher-quality coal beds in the state, and the area's access to the waters of Cook Inlet may mean early development.

The area is already a major energy producer. Chugach Electric Association, one of the major suppliers of power to Anchorage, has tapped the Beluga natural gas fields and operates a gas-fired power plant at Beluga Point north of Tyonek. It is the largest electrical power generating plant in the state. There is talk of developing geothermal energy on Mt. Spurr, an active volcano in the Tordrillo Mountains. Finally, offshore oil rigs in Cook Inlet supply the Drift River oil terminal with raw crude, pumped onto tankers for shipment to the lower 48 states.

Most of the Alaska Range was uninhabitable, although the Athabascan Indians did pass through them, and no doubt hunted in them on occasion. Since most travel was along the coast, the higher mountains remained *terra incognita* until only a hundred years ago. The first white men to record passing through the range were in the Allen Expedition of 1885. Lt. Henry Allen and two other soldiers, Frederick Fickett and Cady Robertson, along with two miners, John Bremmer and Peter Johnson, embarked on a 1,500-mile journey for five months, which took them from Cordova on Prince William Sound north all the way the Koyukuk in the Brooks Range. During their journey they passed from the Copper River drainage via the Slana River to the Tanana drainage crossing Suslota Pass in the Alaska Range. The normally

reserved Allen was overwhelmed by the vastness of the scene before him. He wrote, "The views in advance and rear were both grand, the former showing the extensive Tanana Valley with numerous lakes and the low unbroken range of mountains between the Tanana and Yukon Rivers….I sat proud of the grand sight which no visitor save an Atnatana or Tanana Indian had ever seen." After moving through the pass, they followed the Tok River to the Tanana River and floated it down to the Yukon.

Shortly after the Allen expedition, gold miners began to penetrate the interior of Alaska. Most of the early strikes were on the Yukon or its tributaries, but later miners spread out into the mountain headwaters and made gold discoveries at Chistochina, Kantishna, Yentna, Peters Hills and Hatcher Pass in the Talkeetna Mountains. Other than miners, market hunters and a few adventurers, the Alaska Range has seen little in the way of human development or settlement.

Above: *Meltwater runs down the surface of a glacier in the Alaska Range within Denali National Park.* GEORGE WUERTHNER
Left: *Climbers above Southeast Fork of Kahiltna Glacier in the Alaska Range near Mts. Hunter and Foraker.* BRIAN OKONEK
Facing page, left: *Mt. Kimball portion of the eastern Alaska Range seen from the Mentasta Range.* GEORGE WUERTHNER
Right: *Tundra pond and the Alaska Range in autumn color near milepost 75, Denali National Park.* JAMES RANDKLEV

BROOKS RANGE

The crest of the Brooks Range stretches across northern Alaska for 720 sinewy miles between the Yukon Territory on the east and the coast of the Chukchi Sea on the west. Flanked on the north by the coastal plain known as the North Slope, and hemming in the boreal forestlands of the Kobuk and the Yukon tributaries like the Koyukuk on the south, the entire range lies north of the Arctic Circle. This is Alaska's northernmost mountain range.

Over its vast length, the Brooks Range varies considerably in terrain from gently rolling hills of less than 4,000' at the western end to steep, rugged peaks above 9,000' in elevation in the eastern portion. The Arctic Divide, the northern continuation of the Continental Divide, separates waters draining into the Yukon River from those flowing into the Arctic Ocean.

The Brooks Range is named for Alfred Brooks, a wide-ranging geologist with the U.S. Geological Survey in Alaska around the turn of the century. Although Brooks explored much of Alaska, he never ventured into his namesake mountains.

Beginning near the Yukon Territory border, the Brooks Range is considered by many geologists to be a northern extension of the Rocky Mountain system. The range is divided into a number of sub-units. From east to west there are the Davidson, Romanzof, Sadlerochit, Shublik, Philip Smith, Endicott, Schwatka, Baird and De Long mountains.

No matter what the individual ranges are called, the entire mountain uplift is unified by a common geological history. During the late Jurassic, about 160 million years ago, an ocean plate in the Arctic Ocean rotated counter-clockwise from its original alignment near the High Arctic Islands of northern Canada and began pushing against northern Alaska, driving up mountains. The southern edge of this compressed plate margin now lies along the Kobuk River. Here slices of sedimentary rocks were ripped off a subducting slab of oceanic plate and stacked along the south slope of the Brooks Range. Part of this scraped-off plate material included the massive copper deposits found between Walker Lake and Kiana, which probably represent mineralization associated with old volcanics. North of this suture zone are sedimentary rocks, some of which have been metamorphosed; in places granitic intrusions are found, such as at the Arrigetch Peaks. The oldest rocks lie on the south slope of the Brooks Range and some of these metamorphic greenstone, schists and quartzites are nearly a half billion years in age.

Much of the main crest of the range is composed of limestone that originally was coral reef growing in a tropical sea. Mixed with these limestones are layers of other sedimentary rocks, like the sandstones that hold the Prudhoe Bay oil and the impervious layers of shale that trapped these petroleum deposits. All these sedimentary layers have been tilted, so that they are visibly on-end, and give the mountains along the Arctic Divide a sawtooth appearance. In structure, and even in terms of rock type, they greatly resemble the Rocky Mountain Front in Montana and the Front Ranges of the Canadian Rockies.

Facing page: *Looking southeast from a creek between Amiloyak and Chandler Lake in the Brooks Range.*
BRIAN OKONEK

highest peaks include Mt. Isto (9,050'), Mt. Chamberlin (9,020'), Mt. Hubley (8,915') and Mt. Michelson (8,855'). Glaciers mantle each of these four peaks. The runoff from the glaciers on Mt. Chamberlin feeds Peters and Schrader lakes—the only large lakes fed by glaciers in northern Alaska. The rugged peaks in these mountains consist of limestones, granites and volcanics.

The central portion of the Brooks Range is dominated by the Philip Smith and Endicott mountains. These peaks are slightly lower than the Franklin and Romanzof mountains, but still rugged. Most of the Philip Smith Mountains are within the Arctic Wildlife Refuge, while the Endicott Mountains make up most of the Gates of the Arctic National Park. All the higher peaks in these two ranges average between 6,000' and 8,000'. The Trans-Alaska Pipeline Haul Road passes through Atigun Pass, marking the general boundary between these ranges.

This entire region is made up of two major rock belts. The mountains close to the Arctic Divide are limestone—a rock common through-out the Brooks Range. South of these limestone formations, a severely folded schist belt contains gold-bearing quartz veins. These veins provide the source of gold mined at Wiseman, Chandalar and elsewhere along the south slope of the mountains.

Lying west of the Alatna River and along the divide between the headwaters of the Noatak and Kobuk rivers, the Schwatka Mountains were named for Lt. Frederick Schwatka, the Army officer who first floated the Yukon River all the way from its headwaters to its mouth.

The Schwatka Mountains contain the Arri-getch Peaks, which rank as the most dramatic peaks of the western Brooks Range, perhaps the most dramatic in all Alaska. Like their lofty

All the higher peaks were glaciated during previous ice ages, when a massive glacial system some 500 miles long and 150 miles wide covered most of the range. A smaller glacial system of 120 by 50 miles was centered on the De Long Mountains. These mountains bear the evidence of glaciation in their numerous cirques, arêtes, glacially-carved lakes and U-shaped valleys. Today, despite its northern location, the Brooks Range retains relatively little glacial ice. The general aridity of the climate means there is little snow to form new glacial ice. Most existing glaciers are small ice bodies in north-facing cirques, with the largest no more than five miles in length.

The limited number of glaciers results in clear watercourses, because little glacial flour exists to sully the stream water. Nevertheless, since nearly all of the range is underlain by permafrost, run-off from even modest rains swells the rivers dramatically and can change mild, clear streams into raging torrents overnight. This, combined with the rapid melt-off each spring due to nearly 24 hours of sunlight, creates the braided riverbeds so common here.

As might be expected with a mountain range of such breadth, the characters of individual sub-ranges vary somewhat. The Romanzof and Franklin mountains are the heart of the 18.5-million-acre Arctic Wildlife Refuge. Here the range attains its greatest width, 110 miles, and the coastal plain is at its narrowest. Rising nearly 7,000' above the northern foothills, the counterparts in the Franklin and Romanzof mountains, the Arrigetch Peaks are composed primarily of granite. The severely glaciated Arrigetch region is dominated by pinnacle after knife-edged pinnacle, standing on end in a spectacular procession, with smooth walls rising 3,000' directly from their bases. Seeing them, it is easy to understand why the Eskimos named these peaks Arrigetch, meaning "fingers of the hand extended." The Arrigetch Peaks and nearby Walker Lake are both registered National Natural Landmarks.

Nearly as impressive as the Arrigetch Peaks is 8,570' Mt. Igikpak, highest peak in the western Brooks Range, which lies at the headwaters of the Noatak. The double-turreted summit of Igikpak is cut by a swirl of razor-edged ridges and draped with small glaciers.

Just west of Igikpak the Schwatka Mountains grade into the Baird Mountains, a relatively gentle range rarely exceeding 4,000', with the highest peak only 4,760' in elevation. Named for American naturalist Spencer Fullerton Baird, for whom the Baird sandpiper also is named, the Baird Mountains are composed primarily of folded sedimentary rocks such as sandstone, shale, conglomerate and some metamorphosed limestone, with intruded granites and volcanic rocks. Jade is found in a small area of the Baird Mountains north of Ambler called the Jade Mountains. This rock is transported in winter by sled to Kotzebue, where it is cut and fashioned into jewelry. Even a few small coal deposits crop out along the Kobuk River between Kiana and the Pah River. Most of the higher peaks bear evidence of glaciation, including U-shaped valleys and cirques.

To the north of the Noatak River lie the De Long Mountains. These mountains have glaciated ridges rising to nearly 4,900' with

relief of as much as 3,000' from the surrounding lowlands. They eventually drop in elevation on the west, where they are called the Mulgrave Hills. These predominantly limestone and shale mountains are gentler in nature and lack the high peaks of the central and eastern ends of the range. None of the De Longs rises above 5,000' and most peaks do not even approach 4,000'.

Throughout the Brooks Range there are three district vegetation groupings: tundra, boreal forest and shrub thicket. Lying on the south slope of the range are the northern outliers of the boreal forest. Stringers of spruce-hardwood forest follow rivers deep into the mountains, ending at timberline around 2,100'. Despite their northern location, some of the

Above: *The Brooks Range was named for geologist Alfred Brooks, who explored elsewhere in Alaska, but never here.* **Facing page:** *Sunshine highlights talus slopes along Grizzly Creek in the Endicott Mountains, Gates of the Arctic National Park.* GEORGE WUERTHNER PHOTOS

Above: *Looking southwest from Coldfoot Hill.* CHARLES E. KAY
Facing page: *Looking up the Alatna from a 3,660' peak in the Brooks Range.* BRIAN OKONEK

Except for a few isolated groves of balsam poplar, no trees grow north of the Arctic Divide. Most of these groves are associated with warm springs. The grove at Shublik Spring on Cache Creek, a tributary of the Canning River, probably has the most northerly trees in Alaska.

The climate of the North Slope is considerably different from that of areas south of the Arctic Divide. The north side of the range has an arctic climate. Mean annual temperatures are lower than south of the range and precipitation is extremely light—less than three to five inches a year on the northern parts of the Arctic Wildlife Refuge near the Yukon border.

The region south of the divide has a more continental climate with cold winters and warm summers. Temperatures in the 85° to 90° range are not unusual. For example, the village of Kobuk has recorded a temperature of 92°. Winters are very cold, with a record of minus 68° recorded for Kobuk, minus 65° at Wiseman and the Alaska record of minus 81° recorded at Coldfoot on the South Fork of the Koyukuk. Areas along the coast typically have slightly warmer winters, but cooler summers. Kotzebue's record low is "only" minus 52°. Precipitation diminishes as you move east from the Bering Sea. Precipitation around the Arrigetch Peaks near the headwaters of the Kobuk and Noatak rivers registers about 18" annually, while in the Mt. Doonerak area along the North Fork of the Koyukuk, the total is only about 12". Mean annual temperature at Anaktuvuk Pass (2,200') on the Arctic Divide is 14°, with annual precipitation of 10". More than half the yearly precipitation falls during the summer months.

In general, wildlife is the same on both sides of the range and from east to west, although there are notable exceptions. Black bears inhabit only the forested valleys south of the

white spruce stands have relatively large individuals. I have seen trees along the upper Kobuk easily 18" in diameter, even though tree growth ended only a few miles farther north.

Near timberline, the boreal forest gives way to a shrub thicket community that contains alder, willow, dwarf and resin birch. Birch usually dominates the drier sites, while alder is more common in moist locations.

Above the shrub level is alpine tundra dominated by moss campion, saxifrage, lichens, dryas, dwarf willows, heather and various sedges and grasses. Moist tundra, dominated by cottongrass tussocks forming knee-high clumps, occurs throughout the wetter foothill sites, which makes hiking a nightmare.

range, while grizzlies roam throughout these mountains. But the Brooks Range is marginal grizzly habitat and their numbers are extremely low—approximately one bear per 100 square miles, compared to one bear per square mile in a place like Admiralty Island in Southeast Alaska. Brooks Range grizzlies also tend to be smaller than grizzlies elsewhere, with the average adult male weighing 400 pounds compared to extremely large grizzlies from Kodiak Island and elsewhere that reach weights of 1,400 pounds.

Low reproductive activity hampers the population numbers of Brooks Range bears. Most females do not have their first cubs until they are seven years of age and they may be 10 years or older (in good habitat, females may have cubs at age five). On the average, Brooks Range sows have litters every four years, while in high-quality habitat a female may have cubs every other year. For all these reasons, the grizzlies in the Brooks Range can sustain only very limited human-caused mortality.

Moose are more abundant south of the Arctic Divide but do range onto the North Slope in willow-lined river bottoms.

Dall sheep are spread from the Yukon border nearly to the Chukchi Sea in the western De Long Mountains. For some reason, Dall sheep are not found in the western end of the Baird Mountains. The density of Dall sheep is much lower than in, say, the Wrangell Mountains, probably due to harsh climatic conditions this far north. As with the grizzly, it takes longer for a Brooks Range Dall sheep to reach maturity, compared to sheep growing in more favorable habitat farther south. Males attain full-curl status at around seven years in the more productive Wrangell Mountains, but take 10 to 12 years to achieve a full curl in the Brooks Range.

Several large caribou herds wander through the Brooks Range, each named for its location. There are Western Arctic, Central Arctic and Porcupine herds. The best known is the Porcupine herd, so named because it winters near the Porcupine River in the Yukon Territory. Through time, these various herds change dramatically in numbers and range. For example, during the 1930s, large numbers of caribou wintered in the Yukon Flats, where few if any winter today.

Caribou migrate and, in general, all Brooks Range herds follow a similar seasonal pattern. They spend winters south of the range in spruce forests, where they paw through the snow to find lichens and other foods. They begin a northward migration in March, with females and yearlings preceding the bulls, who follow later. Calving occurs in late May and early June, usually on traditional calving grounds. The Porcupine herd, for example, calves on the coastal plain south of Barter Island within the Arctic Wildlife Refuge. Summers usually are spent in northern foothills or on the North Slope, followed by autumn migrations south to their winter range. The herds usually travel through low passes such as Anaktuvuk, Howard and others.

For countless decades, the caribou, particularly those herds migrating along the coast, provided food for Eskimo people on the north and western edges of the range and for

Athabascan Indians living on the south side of these mountains. Archaeological evidence of these hunting people is spread throughout the range, but one of the best sites in all Alaska is Onion Portage on the Kobuk River. Here generations of hunters have waited in ambush for the passage of the caribou. But many of these sites indicate temporary hunting camps, not year-round occupation and it would be a mistake to believe that these mountains were always inhabited. Until 1400 A.D. it seems the Eskimos moved up the Kobuk River only to winter, and each summer they returned to the ocean to hunt sea mammals. Around this time, about the same time that Columbus was sailing to North America, Eskimo technology grew to

include hook-and-line fishing equipment as well as the sinew-backed bow, which allowed Eskimos to hunt caribou more effectively.

With the bow and arrow, dog teams and effective fishing equipment, some coastal Eskimos began to live year-round in the Brooks Range, taking up a nomadic lifestyle based on hunting caribou. When the first whites entered the Brooks Range in the 1880s, a number of Eskimo groups lived year-round in the mountains but, by 1900, most had abandoned the area to live on the coast where trading opportunities with whites were greater. These people, along with the Eskimos who had always lived on the coast, gradually gravitated towards villages, usually near trading posts and

churches, and gave up their nomadic lifestyle. Then, in 1938, a small number of families moved back to the mountains to resume their old way of life. Yet, a short 10 years later, even most of these people settled more or less permanently in a village at Anaktuvuk Pass, with the last family giving up its nomadic lifestyle in 1960.

Although Eskimos dominated the western Brooks Range and the North Slope, the southern fringes of the Brooks Range in the Koyukuk and Chandalar drainages were predominantly settled by Athabascan Indians. They had been enemies for generations, but Eskimos and Indians along the Koyukuk River managed to live and trade together without a great deal of animosity. On the Koyukuk River both groups live side by side today, with the village of Alatna settled by Eskimos while Allakaket across the river is predominantly Indian. The Indians, like the inland Eskimos, caught salmon and hunted caribou and moose.

Exploration of the Brooks Range came fairly late. The first whites ventured here only about a century ago, when two military men, George Stoney and John Cantwell, launched separate expeditions up the Kobuk in 1884. Stoney went as far as Lake Selby, while Cantwell turned back at the Pah River. The following summer the two men returned. Cantwell went all the way to Walker Lake, thus finding the head-waters of the Kobuk. Stoney and his men spent the winter at a camp they named Fort Cosmos, from which they launched exploratory trips to the Noatak and Alatna rivers. One member of Stoney's party, Ensign W.L. Howard, left Fort Cosmos in April 1886 and traveled overland to Point Barrow, which he reached in August. Howard Pass, where Howard traversed the De Long Mountains, commemorates this man.

At the same time that Stoney and Cantwell were exploring the western Brooks Range, another remarkable officer, Lt. Henry Allen of the Army, became the first white to explore the Koyukuk River in the central Brooks Range. Prospectors later named the Allen River, a tributary of the John River, for Lt. Allen.

A few prospectors and explorers were in the Brooks Range during the 1880s, but not until the turn of the century was much of the range thoroughly explored. Many of the miners who rushed to the Klondike in 1898 later spread out across Alaska looking for placer discoveries. About a thousand of these disappointed miners ascended the Koyukuk in 1898. A half dozen "towns" sprang up in the central Brooks Range along the Middle and South forks of the Koyukuk, including Jimtown, Arctic City, Soo City, Peavy and Union City. That same year about 1,200 prospectors made their way up the Kobuk River—including Robert Bird Grinnell, later famous as a naturalist, for whom Grinnell Glacier in Glacier National Park, Montana is named.

Most of these men left after one winter, but a few did remain and they did find gold. When gold was discovered on Nolan Creek in 1909, the new community of Wiseman was founded; it has survived to this day. The town of Bettles, now called Old Bettles, was founded at the mouth of the John River in 1900 by prospector and miner Gordon Bettles. Bettles marked the end of navigable steamboat travel. To reach Wiseman, upstream, all goods had to be dragged by horse-drawn scows or boats.

In the summer of 1899, the upper Koyukuk attracted USGS geologist Frank C. Schrader (for whom Schrader Lake in the Arctic Wildlife Refuge is named), I.G. Gerdine (commemorated by a peak in the Tordrillo Mountains),

Top: The Kobuk River with the Baird Mountains in the distance. GEORGE WUERTHNER

Above: Golden leaves of balsam poplar against red bearberry in August mark the early arrival of autumn in the Brooks Range. GEORGE WUERTHNER

Left: At St. Michael in September 1886, explorers (left to right) Lt. Frederick Fickett, Lt. Henry Allen and Sgt. Cady Robertson. HISTORICAL PHOTOGRAPH COLLECTION (ACC. #72-164-1) IN THE ARCHIVES, ALASKA AND POLAR REGIONS DEPT., UNIVERSITY OF ALASKA, FAIRBANKS *Facing page:* Along the Kugrak River near the headwaters of the Noatak River in the Schwatka Mountains. GEORGE WUERTHNER

Above: Within the largely sedimentary rocks of the Brooks Range, the rugged granite spires of the Arrigetch Peaks of the Schwatka Mountains represent an anomaly. Arrigetch is an Eskimo word meaning "fingers extended." GEORGE WUERTHNER
Facing page, top: Forester and wilderness supporter Bob Marshall explored the central Brooks Range during the 1930s. He advocated creation of a huge wilderness preserve encompassing everything north of the Yuokon River, including the entire Brooks Range. Although his dream never materialized, today a portion of the Brooks Range is protected within the Gates of the Arctic National Park. UNIVERSITY OF CALIFORNIA AT BERKELEY
Bottom: Reeds in tundra pond near Chandler Lake in the Endicott Mountains, Gates of the Arctic National Park. GEORGE WUERTHNER

and D.C. Witherspoon (who had a peak in the Chugach Mountains named after him) mapped portions of the Koyukuk and Chandalar rivers. In 1901, Schrader was back, this time with W.J. Peters (for whom Peters Lake in the Arctic Wildlife Refuge is named), and the party ascended the John River, crossing the Brooks Range at the low pass now known as Anaktuvuk. They descended the Anaktuvuk River to the Beaufort Sea, thus becoming the first white party to cross the central part of the range.

A few years later, in 1910, USGS geologist Philip S. Smith (for whom the Philip Smith Mountains are named) explored the upper Kobuk River. The next summer he was back on the Koyukuk, which he followed up to the Alatna River. Smith ascended the Alatna, then crossed Portage Pass to the Noatak and descended the entire length of that stream.

During the 1920s, life settled to a steady pace in the central Brooks Range as a small corps of miners worked the gold fields. In 1929, a romantic but energetic young forester named Robert Marshall traveled to Alaska to explore the central Brooks Range. He was probably one of the first people to come to the Brooks Range strictly to see its wild country. At that time, no place was wilder than the headwaters of the Koyukuk.

Between 1929 and 1939, Marshall made four trips to the Koyukuk and wintered one year at Wiseman. He reveled in the life of an explorer, traveling up drainages where few had ventured, and he made one of the most complete maps of the region. It was Marshall who bestowed the name "Gates of the Arctic" upon the twin peaks that hem in the North Fork of the Koyukuk near its confluence with Ernie Creek. He wrote two books about his experiences in the Brooks Range: *Arctic Village*, which described life in Wiseman during the 1930s, and *Alaska Wilderness*, which detailed his exploratory trips in the mountains.

Marshall's enthusiasm for wilderness was unbounded and, as a forester with the U.S. Forest Service and with the Bureau of Indian Affairs, Marshall constantly worked to preserve of wild land. In 1935, he helped found the Wilderness Society. Stimulated by his travels in the Brooks Range, the visionary Marshall advocated making the entire northern half of Alaska from the Yukon River to the Arctic Ocean into one large wilderness preserve. Although a scheme as grandiose as Marshall's never developed, designation of the Gates of the Arctic National Park and Preserve can be attributed partly to the publicity that resulted from his books. Marshall Lake below Mt. Doonerak on the North Fork of the Koyukuk was named to honor this man.

In recognition of the region's superb ecological and scenic values, practically the entire range from the Yukon Border to the Chukchi Sea is within some conservation area. From east to west are the 18.5-million-acre Arctic National Wildlife Refuge, the 8-million-acre Gates of the Arctic National Park and Preserve, the 6.5-million-acre Noatak Preserve and the 1.7-million-acre Kobuk Valley National Park encompassing part of the Baird Mountains. Finally, the 540,000-acre Cape Krusenstern National Monument takes in a portion of the Mulgrave Hills west of the Noatak River.

The De Long and Baird mountains, along with the Schwatka Mountains, cradle the 435-mile-long Noatak River drainage, an area within the Noatak Preserve. This is a designated biosphere reserve under the United Nations' Man and the Biosphere program which seeks to identify relatively pristine ecosystems world-wide, as controls against which ecosystems influenced by humans can be monitored.

Areas outside the preserves are open to mineral development and both the De Long and Baird mountains have major mineral deposits of international importance. Two recent discoveries include the Red Dog and Lik lead-zinc-silver deposits in the De Long Mountains. Open-pit mines operated by NANA Native Corporation soon will be tapping these mineral outcrops. In addition, a massive 150-mile-long sulfide copper belt runs along the Kobuk River between Walker Lake and Kiana in the Baird Mountains. During the 1970s, competing mining companies staked

more than 10,000 claims as they attempted to define what many considered one of the richest copper belts in the world. The most promising regions between the Gates of the Arctic and Kobuk Valley national parks were purposely excluded from those conservation areas to allow for future development. NANA, in cooperation with several international mining corporations, likely will operate mines in this region once the prices of the mineral rises sufficiently.

THE YUKON

There are a number of low mountain ranges in the upper Yukon River drainage, including the White Mountains of the Yukon-Tanana uplands, Ray Mountains and the Ogilvie Mountains that barely enter Alaska east of the Nation River and in the upper Tatonduk River drainage along the Alaska-Yukon border.

Overall the area was not glaciated during the great Ice Ages, although the higher peaks do exhibit some cirques and arêtes carved by small glaciers.

Four major terranes make up this portion of Alaska, each sequentially tacked onto Alaska after being formed elsewhere. From Fairbanks east to the Yukon border, including the White Mountains and the highlands along the Fortymile River, stretches part of the Yukon-Tanana terrane. Most of the Yukon-Tanana terrane is composed of metamorphic rocks, primarily schists, but there are sedimentary rocks such as limestone, and even coal and oil shales. The schists contain a great deal of gold, explaining so many gold strikes here, including the placer deposits at Circle, on the Fortymile River and near Fairbanks. These rocks are some of the oldest exposed in Alaska, some 600 to 800 million years in age.

Intruded into these old schists are younger granitic plutons. Radioactive decay in these granitic rocks produces sufficient heat to warm water circulating in deep cracks. Some of this water flows out on the surface as hot springs, including Chena and Circle hot springs.

North of the Yukon-Tanana terrane is the Manley terrane, formed primarily of lavas and sedimentary rocks. The outcrops of granite account for the presence of Manley Hot Spring. Serpentinized peridotite, which usually occurs deep in the mantle, is found here. Formed when a subducting plate scrapes onto a continental plate margin, peridotite has a greenish appearance and soapy feel.

The Tozitna terrane just north of the Yukon River, by Livengood, is composed of basalt, sandstone, limestone, conglomerate, tuff (rock made of volcanic ash) and gabbro (rock similar to granite). The northernmost terrane is the Ruby, composed of schist and gneiss as well as granite. Most of the Ray Mountains are part of this terrane.

The Yukon-Tanana uplands include the rugged limestone outcrops in both the White Mountains drained by Beaver Creek north of the Steese Highway and unnamed highlands south and east of the Steese Highway drained by the Salcha River, Goodpaster River, Birch Creek, Fortymile River and Charley River. This dissected plateau features gently rolling ridgelines interspersed with steep hillsides that drop to the river bottoms. The highest peaks top out at around 6,000′ elevation. Among the named higher peaks are: 5,784′ Twin Mountain along the Charley River, 6,250′ Mt. Eldridge and 5,743′ Glacier Mountain near the headwaters of Mission Creek near Eagle, 6,543′ Mt. Harper at the headwaters of the Middle Fork of the Fortymile and 5,547′ Mt. Fairplay along the Taylor Highway. The White Mountains include 4,772′ Cache Mountain, 5,062′ Lime Peak and 5,286′ Mt. Prindle.

Facing page: The Ogilvie Mountains seen beyond the Tatonduck River in Yukon-Charley National Park.
GEORGE WUERTHNER

Some of this landscape is federally protected, including the 2,260,000-acre Yukon-Charley Preserve, the million-acre White Mountains National Recreation Area and the 375-mile corridor of the Fortymile River, designated a Wild and Scenic River.

North of the Tintina Fault, which lies along the Yukon River, is an area thought to be an eroding continental margin. East of the Nation River to the Yukon border, sedimentary rocks unaltered by metamorphism, represent a 620-million-year time span. The highest peaks are barely over 4,000' and the only named peak of any height on the Alaska side of the U.S.-Canada border is 3,440' Three Castle Mountain (just across in the Yukon Territory, the Ogilvie Mountains rise to 6,000'). Excellent outcrops of fossilized limestones appear at places like Calico Bluff along the Yukon River. Some of these sedimentary rocks contain oil reserves and the largest are found along the Kandik River and east to the Yukon border.

South of the Tintina Fault, in the area drained by the Fortymile River, a mixture of metamorphic and sedimentary rocks includes limestone, marble, sandstone, shale and conglomerate. Birch Creek schist, common throughout the Yukon-Tanana uplands, also characterizes this drainage. Intrusions of granite occur and granites and rhyolite make up the bulk of Mt. Fairplay, an ancient volcano, which travelers on the Taylor Highway cross. The occurrence of asbestos at Slate Creek in the North Fork of the Fortymile indicates that a portion of mantle material from deep in the earth was scraped onto the edge of the growing continental plate margin during a subduction sequence long ago.

Most of this region was unglaciated by the last Ice Age, although a few of the highest

peaks, such as Glacier Mountain southwest of Eagle, do show some signs of glaciation—including small cirques and moraines. And rare plants found on dry slopes along the Yukon River represent relics of the steppe-tundra grasslands widespread over much of interior Alaska during the Ice Age. Some of these are *Crypatantha shackletteana*, *Erigonum flavum*, *Erysimum asperum* and *Podistera yukonensis*.

The lack of alpine glaciated terrain means Dall sheep are relatively restricted in distribution, occurring only along the Charley River, at Glacier Mountain, and along the Yukon border in the Ogilvie Mountains. The Ogilvies are the only place where the Fannin color phase, a gray-brown variety of Dall sheep, occurs in Alaska.

Most mammals typical of Alaska's interior inhabit the upper Yukon, including caribou, wolf, grizzly bear, black bear, moose, hoary marmot, collared pika, wolverine, river otter, weasel, mink and beaver.

The region along the upper Yukon—including such rivers as the Fortymile, Charley, Kandik and Tatonduk—supports one of the highest densities of peregrine falcons nesting in North America. At least 28 occupied nests exist within the Yukon-Charley Preserve alone.

The Ray Mountains lie in the heart of Alaska between the Koyukuk and Yukon rivers. The highest peaks in these rolling, seldom-visited mountains include 5,519' Mt. Tozi and 4,827' Mt. Henry Eakin. Much of the range is composed of schists, with outcrops of granite and gneiss bedrock that have eroded into pinnacles and tors as high as 90'. One such area abundant with these granitic outcrops is known as Spooky Valley. Only the highest peaks were glaciated, and they are marked by cirques, horns, U-shaped valleys and other glacial

features. Two small hot springs evidence the granitic plutons.

Interestingly, no Dall sheep inhabit the Ray Mountains, although nearly all other large mammals typical of the interior of Alaska do. Recent research for the first time found marmots in the Ray Mountains.

Most of the highlands above 2,000' are dominated first by dwarf shrub forest, then alpine tundra. The bottomlands consist of mixed spruce-hardwood forest, which includes white spruce, paper birch, aspen, black spruce and balsam poplar. Wildfires are common and no place in the interior of Alaska has not burned at least once in the past 200 years.

Above: *Gold strikes on Birch Creek in 1893 led to the founding of Circle. Interior reaches of Alaska remained virtually unknown until the discovery of gold in paying quantities on the Fortymile River in 1886 brought miners into the region.* HEGG NEG. 909, SPECIAL COLLECTIONS, UNIVERSITY OF WASHINGTON
Facing page, top: *An abandoned gold dredge on the Walker Fork.* GEORGE WUERTHNER
Bottom: *A hiker views the Middle Fork of the Fortymile River, a designated Wild and Scenic River, as it flows through the rolling Yukon Highlands, an area never glaciated, even during the height of the Ice Age.* GEORGE WUERTHNER

Left to right:
Peregrine falcon. KENNAN WARD
At the World Eskimo & Indian Olympics in Fairbanks.
RON SANFORD
The sternwheeler Discovery III *on the Tanana River near Fairbanks.* RON SANFORD

The climate is continental, with very cold winters and hot summers. Annual precipitation is light—Fairbanks gets only 10″, Fort Yukon 7″, Eagle near the Yukon border 11″. Thunderstorms are common in summer, when most annual precipitation occurs. In winter, temperatures may dip to 60° or 70° below zero, but wind-chill is not a problem. The lack of wind does contribute to temperature inversions—which tend to trap air pollution in the valleys as "ice fog"—and cities like Fairbanks suffer horrendous smog on cold winter days.

In this harsh climatic regime lived scattered bands of Athabascan Indians. Estimates put the entire Indian population of the Yukon basin at no more than 7,000 people at the time of contact with whites. Hunting big game like moose and caribou, catching salmon on the Yukon and its tributaries, these people were highly nomadic and lived in small family groups because the land would not support large concentrations of people.

The first whites ventured into the region from Canada when Robert Campbell of the Hudson's Bay Company built a trading post in 1847 at Fort Yukon.

In 1865, Robert Kennicott led a party surveying the route for a telegraph line up the

94

Yukon. When Kennicott died, William Dall took over as leader. An advance party under Fran Ketchum and Michael LaBarge (for whom Lake LaBarge in the Yukon Territory is named) proceeded up the Yukon into the Yukon Territory. Dall followed, making observations, and the parties reunited at Fort Yukon. The telegraph project was abandoned when a transatlantic cable was completed, but Dall and his party succeeded in making one of the first accurate maps of the Yukon River in Alaska.

In 1873, a few miners began exploring the Yukon basin. Among the first were Leroy McQuesten (for whom the McQuesten River in the Yukon Territory is named) and Arthur Harper (for whom Mt. Harper near the headwaters of the Fortymile is named). Neither miner found large quantities of gold, but each found enough to keep his interest. Then, in 1886, gold was found in paying quantities on the Fortymile River. This precipitated the first gold rush to the interior of Alaska. In 1893, gold was reported on Birch Creek and, by 1896, more than a thousand prospectors were exploring the Yukon and its tributaries in Alaska. But it was the news of gold on the Klondike River in the Yukon Territory in 1897 that caused the great gold rush of 1898, when more than 100,000 people came north looking for the yellow metal. Many of the old mining camps are nothing more than ruins today, although a few like Circle, Fairbanks, Livengood and Eagle have managed to hang on as regional trade centers.

The interior of Alaska was a particularly good place to look for gold, since glaciation had not disturbed the rivers or ancient river terraces that held placer deposits. Few discoveries were lode deposits, but millions of dollars in placer gold was taken from the region's streams and

rivers. Even today, gold mining continues on such streams as Birch Creek, the Fortymile River and Woodchopper Creek.

The Washington-Alaska Military Cable and Telegraph System, constructed in 1903, linked Fort Egbert at Eagle with Valdez and eventually Washington, D.C. It is still possible to find the old telegraph line and tripods crossing the mountains between Eagle and Tok, along with several of the old line-maintenance cabins.

Above: Clouds lit at sunset along the Charley River. Summers in the Interior are frequently hot, and lighning storms are common.
Left: The old roadhouse at Steel Creek along the Fortymile River recalls gold rush days when the human population of the Yukon Highlands peaked. In essence, this region is more a wilderness now than it was a hundred years ago.
GEORGE WUERTHNER PHOTOS

WESTERN RANGES

Western Alaska, as a whole, contains the least impressive mountains in the state. Much of the region is relatively flat, generally wet and not awe-inspiring. The Yukon-Kuskokwim delta is a 250-by-200-mile expanse of wetlands—great for ducks but lacking in the scenic qualities most people find elsewhere in Alaska. Other lowlands and flats stretch along the Selawik River, at Dulbi Flats and along the northern edge of the Seward Peninsula.

Rolling hills or mountains cover the rest of the region, but few peaks exceed even 5,000'. For this reason, most of these mountains are little-known, or visited only by people from local communities. The area includes a number of low rolling hills such as the Waring Mountains, Zane Hills, Purcell Mountains and Lockwood Hills, which lie between the Kobuk River and Koyukuk drainages. The Kigluaik, Bendeleben, Darby and York mountains occupy the Seward Peninsula, while the Nulato Hills cradle the west side of the lower Yukon river. East and south of the Yukon are the Kuskokwim Mountains, which run south from the Yukon River near Ruby all the way to Bristol Bay. The Kuskokwims include several named ranges, such as the Kilbuck, Ahklun and Wood River mountains, which form the divide between the Kuskokwim delta country and the waters of Bristol Bay.

Mountains near the sea, as well as nearly all of the Seward Peninsula except the area around Norton Bay, are mostly treeless, covered with tundra. Few trees grow along the lower Yukon or Kuskokwim river near the delta, but the upper regions are heavily forested with spruce-hardwood stands.

The most impressive of these western Alaska mountains are the Wood River, Ahklun and Kilbuck mountains west of Dillingham near Bristol Bay. They are not necessarily higher than the ranges farther north, but they are glacially scoured and chiseled. Their proximity to the ocean meant that extensive ice sheets formed during the Ice Age. The highest of these mountains are the extremely rugged Ahklun Mountains, which range in elevations from sea level to near 5,500'. Mt. Oratia (5,400') near the headwaters of the Kanektok River—which supports the most northerly steelhead trout runs in the world—and 5,026' Mt. Waskey near Togiak Lake are the highest summits. Although only a few small glaciers still clothe Mt. Waskey, these extremely craggy mountains once were covered by extensive ice sheets.

One of the rare geological features of these mountains is the "tuya" found in the Togiak valley. A tuya forms when a volcano erupts under a glacier. The resulting mountain is flat-topped and steep-sided.

Glaciers also account for the broad U-shaped valleys in these mountains, often filled with deep trough-like lakes such as Kanektok, Goodnews and 13-mile-long Togiak. Each of these rivers is world-famous for trophy trout fishing and they also support major salmon fisheries.

This area is a major hard-rock mineral province with deposits of platinum, gold, copper, mercury, palladium and silver. The platinum deposits were discovered in 1926 on the Salmon River near Goodnews Bay by Eskimo prospector Walter Smith. By 1934, the

Facing page: The low, rounded Waring Mountains with a fresh coating of snow, viewed across the Kobuk River.
GEORGE WUERTHNER

Goodnews Bay Mining Company had acquired most of these claims and in 1937 began dredging operations on the placer deposits. These are still the largest recoverable platinum deposits in Alaska. Gold was first discovered here in 1900 in the Arolik Basin. Other placer deposits were found in the Ahklun Mountains on Olympic, Bear, Rainey, Butte and Tyone creeks.

East of the Ahklun Mountains are the slightly lower (2,000' to 3,500'), but no less rugged, Wood River Mountains, which cradle 11 narrow fiord-like glacial lakes. They form part of the 1.4-million-acre Wood-Tikchik State Park, Alaska's largest state reserve. The lakes and rivers provide abundant spawning and rearing habitat for salmon and these waters make a substantial contribution to the Bristol Bay fisheries, Alaska's largest and most valuable salmon fisheries. These waterways also enjoy world renown as the trophy-trout-fishing capital of Alaska, and numerous fishing lodges dot their shorelines.

To the north of the Ahklun Mountains and southeast of Bethel are the Kilbuck Mountains, drained by the headwaters of the Aniak, Kisaralik and several other short rivers of the lower Kuskokwim. The higher peaks in the Kilbucks are just above 4,000' with Breast Mountain at 4,550' and 3,645' Mt. Hamilton among the highest. Like the Ahklun and Wood River mountains, the Kilbucks also were severely glaciated and are very rugged at higher elevations.

These mountains were named for a Delaware Indian named John Henry Kilbuck, a Moravian missionary in the Kuskokwim delta country. He was well respected among the natives and even more so when he developed blood poisoning in his arm and allowed the limb to be amputated in full view of an Eskimo audience.

This region was settled by Eskimo groups who lived primarily along the coast subsisting, in part, upon the abundant salmon fisheries as well as birds and marine mammals. When Captain Cook entered Goodnews Bay in 1778, he was approached by Eskimos in kayaks. Since they had no articles of foreign manufacture, Cook believed these people had had no previous contact with whites.

It was not until 1818 that Europeans influenced the native groups in this area. The Russians set up a trading post on the Nushagak River and, later, near the mouth of the Togiak River. After the sale of Alaska to the United States, the first salmon canneries were established in Bristol Bay. They rapidly replaced the fur trade in economic importance.

Reindeer herding became popular in this region shortly after the turn of the century, but declined so that, by the 1940s, the herds were gone. At the same time, gold mining, stopped during World War II, never recovered. Today, the Ahklun Mountains and a portion of the southern Kilbuck Mountains are part of the 4.1-million-acre Togiak National Wildlife Refuge, while the western portion of the Kilbuck Mountains are included in the Yukon Delta National Wildlife Refuge.

The Ahklun, Kilbuck and Wood River mountains gradually blend into the Kuskokwim Mountains farther north. These mountains begin just north of the Aniak River and run north to the Yukon River. They represent the most extensive uplands in this region. Gentle mountains, with few evidences of glaciation, the highest peaks are usually less than 4,000'. Some of the higher summits include 4,508' Van Frank Mountain, 3,366' Russian Mountain, 3,229' Holokuk Mountain and 3,595' Twin Mountain.

The Kuskokwim River does not originate in these mountains; rather, its headwaters flow from the western flanks of the Alaska Range. On its way to the Bering Sea it cuts across the Kuskokwim mountains. It is the second-longest river in Alaska, generally a slow and meandering river with an extremely low gradient. For example, the North Fork of the Kuskokwim north of McGrath is only 650' above sea level at its headwaters and in the 250 miles it travels to Stoney River, the river drops only 220'. Since there are no glaciers in the Kuskokwim Mountains, rivers originating within the mountains themselves are generally clear.

A number of the gold discoveries in the Innoko district brought miners to the area in the early 1900s and towns like McGrath sprang up to serve the miners' needs. One of Mc-Grath's claims to fame is that, in 1924, it became the first Alaskan town to receive airmail service. Today the town is a prominent checkpoint on the 1,000-mile Iditarod dog sled race that runs each year between Anchorage and Nome. Another gold-rush community was Ruby along the Yukon River on the northern end of the Kuskokwim Mountains. Major place gold discoveries occurred here in both 1907 and 1911, and a post office was established by 1912.

West of the Yukon River from the Kuskokwim Mountains are the Nulato Hills. Although called hills, these uplands are really no lower than other areas in this region dignified by the name mountains. The higher peaks include 3,411' Debauch Mountain, 2,490' Notakok Mountain and 2,838' Traverse Peak. This gently rolling landscape forms a watershed divide between Norton Sound and the lower Yukon River. One of the major rivers draining these hills is the Unalakleet, a designated Wild and Scenic River. In the days before the airplane, the Kaltag Portage between the Unalakleet drainage and the Yukon was a major transportation link between the interior and the coast.

A number of low mountain ranges occupy the Seward Peninsula, a rocky point of land 200 miles by 120 miles that juts into the Bering Sea, practically touching the mainland of Siberia.

Lowlands cover the northern portion of the peninsula while low rolling hills and gentle mountains cover the southern half. None of these ranges has a peak above 5,000' and most average considerably lower. The peninsula is an uplifted dissected plateau composed primarily of schists and slate with occasional granitic outcrops. No well defined system of ridges or peaks exists, although pinnacles and rocky outcrops abound above a surface that is generally rolling and gentle.

The major mountain areas are the Kigluaik Mountains north of Nome whose highest peak, Mt. Osborn, is 4,714' in elevation. Relative to the rest of the peninsula, this is extremely rugged country, and the local name for this portion of the Kigluaiks is the "Sawtooths."

To the east of the Nome-Taylor Road, the Bendeleben Mountains send peaks above 3,000', with 3,730' Mt. Bendeleben their highest. The Bendeleben Mountains are named for Baron Otto von Bendeleben, who explored the area in 1865 and 1866. Along the headwaters of the Fish River east of Council are the Darby Mountains, whose higher peaks include 2,671' Omilak Mountain, 2,995' Mt. Arathlatuluk and 2,089' Mt. Kachauik. The York Mountains near Cape Prince of Wales include 2,898' Brooks Mountain (named for early USGS geologist Alfred Brooks, for whom the Brooks Range also is named) and Cape Mountain, whose 2,289' summit forms the westernmost tip of the peninsula.

About 20 percent of the peninsula was glaciated during the Ice Age and the highest mountains, particularly in the Bendeleben and Kigluaik mountains, have been extensively glaciated. They are somewhat rugged in appearance, complete with cirques, arêtes and morainal surfaces. But today there are only a

Above: Fly-fishing Lake Beverly in the Wood River Mountains. CHARLIE CRANGLE   **Top:** *The nearby, stormy waters of Bristol Bay were a steady source of moisture for the Wood River Mountains during the last Ice Age, and supported large glaciers here.* ERWIN AND PEGGY BAUER
Facing page: *A number of fiord-like glacial lakes such as Nerka Lake, seen here, divide the Wood River Mountains.* CHARLIE CRANGLE

Above: Autumn color highlights vegetation patterns in the Kuskokwim Mountains southeast of Ruby. Golden paper birches cover the warmer south slopes, while the colder north slopes are dominated by coniferous black spruce.
Facing page: Nulato Hills seen along the Unlakleet River. The Kaltag portage cuts across the Nulato Hills, which separate the Yukon and Unlakleet drainages. The route has been used for centuries as a shortcut from the lower Yukon to Norton Sound. GEORGE WUERTHNER PHOTOS

few small glaciers—all found in the Kigluaik Mountains on or near Mt. Osborn, all rapidly shrinking. When Alfred Brooks explored the Kigluaik Mountains in 1900, he found several glaciers near the head of the North Fork of the Grand Central River. By 1950, when these areas were re-examined, all the glaciers described by Brooks had disappeared. Several other glaciers, including Grand Union Glacier, were found during the 1950s. By the time Grand Union Glacier was revisited in the 1970s, it had shrunk by 50 percent.

Besides glaciation, the other major geologic influence has been volcanism, which began on the peninsula some 65 million years ago, with the most recent activity less than a thousand years ago. Stretching in a line trending southeast to northwest, from the Koyuk River headwaters to Cape Espenberg on Kotzebue Sound, dozens of volcanic vents and several major lava fields resemble the Craters of the Moon region of Idaho. Devil's Mountain within the Bering Land Bridge National Preserve on the northern end of the peninsula was named by Otto Von Kotzebue, who likened the 798' mountain to a ruined castle. The area has many old volcanic craters, and five of the largest explosion calderas now hold lakes, including White Fish Lake, Devil Mountain Lakes and Killeak Lakes. Cinder cones and pumice abound, but lava flows are relatively uncommon.

Another area of major volcanic activity surrounds Lake Imuruk. About 900 square miles of lava flows cover the Imuruk region, some less than a thousand years old. Vents and cones dot the landscape. Most of the flows are of the *pahoehoe* type with small *aa* flows, both of which occur when a basalt crust begins to form on still-flowing lava. When a pahoehoe flow

hardens, the basalt forms rope-like rock in the direction of the flow; in hardened aa flows, the basalt is in chunks that look like ice floes on a re-frozen river.

The Seward Peninsula was one of the first parts of Alaska to be visited by Europeans exploring the coast, but the interior remained virtually unknown for more than a century. Beginning in 1833—when the Russians built a trading post at St. Michael near the mouth of the Yukon—coastal Eskimos began to feel the European influence as trade goods became commonplace. Change intensified after 1848 when the *Superior*, a whaling vessel from New York, passed the tip of the Seward Peninsula and entered the Arctic Ocean in pursuit of bowhead whales. Within two years, more than 149 other whalers were working these waters. The whalers killed whales and walruses, both important food items for local Eskimos. In addition, they brought diseases for which the native people had no immunities. The Eskimos also unwittingly contributed to their own demise by willingly trading caribou meat and other native foods to the whalers in exchange for European trade goods. Eskimos hunting with modern weapons to satisfy a steady demand from the whalers quickly depleted local game populations.

Once the whaling era ended, the Eskimos were left destitute without alternative foods and ridden by disease. Dr. Sheldon Jackson, the General Agent for Education in Alaska, visited the Seward Peninsula Eskimos and decided that the introduction of reindeer might provide a steady food supply for the natives as well as a livelihood. Between 1892 and 1902, some 1,280 reindeer were bought in Siberia and moved to Alaska. Laplanders were hired to teach the Eskimos herding techniques and, by 1914, the entire peninsula was divided among 30 herds. The 1937 Reindeer Act made it illegal for any non-native to own reindeer. Herding has fluctuated since then. In recent years, various Native Corporations have become involved in herding and selling antlers for use as an aphrodisiac in the Orient.

Reindeer herding quickly was overshadowed when gold was discovered along Melsing and Ophir creeks near Council in 1898. In September of that same year, gold was discovered near Nome on Anvil Creek. The news of the big strike reached Dawson upstream after the Yukon had frozen. Dawson was full of disappointed gold seekers who had come too late to stake claims on the rich Klondike placers. Most had to wait impatiently for spring so they could descend the Yukon by boat. Some could not wait for spring and left Dawson in mid-winter, traveling over the frozen Yukon by dog sled.

One disappointed Klondiker, afraid he would be too late for yet another gold strike if he waited until spring, was Ed Jesson. Unable to buy dogs, Jesson saw a bicycle in a store in Dawson and purchased it for $150 dollars. After practicing riding on ice for a few days, Jesson took off for Nome. Bicycling appeared to be practical transportation and Jesson was making more than 50 miles a day. He even passed another gold-smitten prospector who was skating from Dawson to Nome. When the temperature dipped to 48° below zero, Jesson had problems keeping his nose from freezing. He had to stop continuously to put a mittened glove to his face to warm it since he couldn't steer his bike with just one hand. One gusty day, the wind threw him into an ice jam and the bicycle's handlebars snapped in the cold air like brittle glass. He carved a new set out of spruce and soon was on his way. A month after

leaving Dawson, Jesson reached Nome in a trip not likely to be repeated.

Jesson's fears that he would be overwhelmed if he waited were not unfounded. By the following fall some 30,000 people had descended on Nome. By chance, one miner dug up some of the beach sand in Nome—only to discover that it, too, contained gold. By late summer a 42-mile stretch of beach was being mined. Other strikes on the Seward Peninsula soon followed and towns sprang up to serve the miners, including Solomon, Dime Landing, Candle, Deering and Haycock. Eventually companies rather than individuals did most of the mining, and at one time more than 100 large dredges worked the gravels and river benches.

North of the Seward Peninsula, another series of low mountains and hills surrounds the Selawik Basin and creates a watershed divide between the Kobuk and Koyukuk drainages. These rolling uplands include the Waring Mountains, Lockwood Hills, Zane Hills, Sheklukshuk Range and Purcell Mountains.

The most northerly are the Waring Mountains, which define the southern rim of part of the Kobuk River valley. The highest peaks are less than 2,000' and their terrain is gently rolling. Lt. George Stoney named the mountains during his 1886 Kobuk River expedition. Composed of conglomerate and sorted basaltic rocks in a mudstone matrix, the Waring Mountains had little geological interest for the miners who explored the Kobuk River in the late 1800s and early 1900s.

To the east of the Waring Mountains, the Lockwood Hills join the Waring Mountains in forming the southern rim of the upper Kobuk Valley. The Lockwood Hills are drained by the Pah River, the only major Kobuk tributary draining from the south. The highest peak is

4,130' Angutikada Peak. Extending in a long ridge angling northwest to southeast are the Sheklukshuk Range and Zane Hills. The highest peak, 4,053' Cone Mountain, is in the southern portion of the Zane Hills.

The Purcell Mountains are another small ridge-like range running east and west along the Continental Divide eventually intercepting the north-south–trending Nulato Hills. The highest point is 3,831' Purcell Mountain. All these mountains are little known and explored. At present few communities exist near them.

ALASKA FACTS

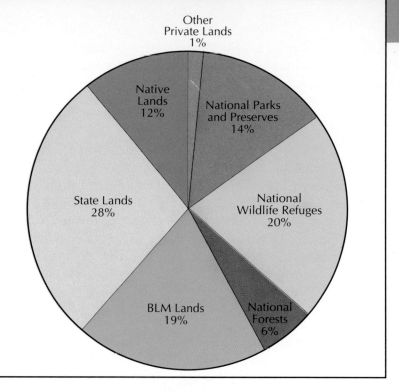

LAND STATUS

- Other Private Lands 1%
- Native Lands 12%
- National Parks and Preserves 14%
- National Wildlife Refuges 20%
- National Forests 6%
- BLM Lands 19%
- State Lands 28%

ALASKA'S WEATHER

CITY	TEMPERATURES				PRECIPITATION
	MEAN HIGH	LOW	RECORD HIGH	LOW	INCHES
ANCHORAGE	42	28	85	-34	15
ATKA	44	36	77	12	60
BARROW	15	4	76	-54	5
BETTLES	30	12	92	-70	14
COLD BAY	42	33	77	-13	35
FAIRBANKS	36	16	96	-62	10
FORT YUKON	31	10	97	-71	7
HOMER	44	30	80	-21	24
JUNEAU	47	33	90	-22	52
KETCHIKAN	52	39	90	-4	156
KOTZEBUE	28	15	85	-52	9
LITTLE PORT WALTER	48	38	78	0	224
NOME	32	18	86	-46	16
NORTHWAY	32	11	91	-72	10
YAKUTAT	45	32	86	-24	133

ALASKA'S MOUNTAIN RANGES

	ELEVATION
AHKLUN MTNS.	1,000-3,000
ALASKA RANGE	to 20,320
ALEUTIAN RANGE	to 10,000
BAIRD MTNS.	to 4,300
BENDELEBEN MTNS.	to 3,730
BROOKS RANGE	4,000-9,000
CHIGMIT MTNS.	to 8,000
CHUGACH MTNS.	to 13,176
COAST MTNS.	to 10,000
DARBY MTNS.	to 3,083
DAVIDSON MTNS.	to 5,540
DE LONG MTNS.	to 4,886
ENDICOTT MTNS.	to 7,000
FAIRWEATHER RANGE	to 15,300
FRANKLIN MTNS.	to 9,000
KAIYUH MTNS.	1,000-2,844
KENAI MTNS.	to 6,000
KILBUCK MTNS.	to 4,714
KUSKOKWIM MTNS.	to 3,973
MENTASTA MTNS.	to 8,500
NULATO HILLS	to 3,500
NUTZOTIN MTNS.	5,000-8,000
PURCELL MTNS.	to 3,500
RAY MTNS.	2,500-5,500
ROMANZOF MTNS.	to 8,700
SAINT ELIAS MTNS.	to 18,000
SCHWATKA MTNS.	to 8,800
TALKEETNA MTNS.	6,000-8,800
WARING MTNS.	to 1,800
WHITE MTNS.	to 5,000
WRANGELL MTNS.	to 16,421
YORK MTNS.	to 2,349
ZANE HILLS	to 4,053

ALASKA'S HIGHEST MOUNTAINS

	ELEVATION
McKINLEY, SOUTH PEAK	20,320
McKINLEY, NORTH PEAK	19,470
SAINT ELIAS	18,008
FORAKER	17,400
BLACKBURN	16,523
BONA	16,421
SANFORD	16,237
SOUTH BUTTRESS	15,885
VANCOUVER	15,700
CHURCHILL	15,638
FAIRWEATHER	15,300
HUBBARD	15,015
BEAR	14,831
EAST BUTTRESS	14,730
HUNTER	14,573
ALVERSTONE	14,565
BROWNE TOWER	14,530
WRANGELL	14,163
AUGUSTA	14,070

SOURCES OF INFORMATION

Bureau of Land Management, U.S. Department of the Interior. Alaska State Office, 701 C St., P.O. Box 13, Anchorage, AK 99513.

National Park Service, U.S. Department of the Interior. Alaska Regional Office, 2525 Gambell St., Anchorage, AK 99503. Phone (907) 261-2643.

Forest Service, U.S. Department of Agriculture. Alaska Regional Office, P.O. Box 1628, Juneau, AK 99802. Phone (907) 586-8806.

U.S. Fish and Wildlife Service, U.S. Department of the Interior. Alaska Area Office, 1011 E. Tudor Rd., Anchorage, AK 99503. (907) 786-3487.

Alaska Division of Parks and Outdoor Recreation, Department of Natural Resources, P.O. Box 7001, Anchorage, AK 99510. Phone (907) 561-2020.

Alaska Department of Fish and Game, P.O. Box 3-2000, Juneau, AK 99802. Phone (907) 465-4180 (Fish); (907) 465-4190 (Game).

AMERICAN GEOGRAPHIC PUBLISHING

EACH BOOK HAS ABOUT 100 PAGES, 11" X 8½", 120 TO 170 COLOR PHOTO-GRAPHS

Enjoy, See, Understand America State by State

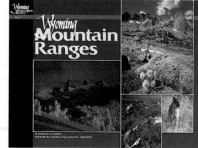

**American Geographic Publishing
Geographic Series of the States**

Lively, colorful, beautifully illustrated books specially written for these series explain land form, animals and plants, economy, lifestyle and history of each state or feature. Generous color photography brings each state to life and makes each book a treat to turn to frequently. The geographic series format is designed to give you more information than coffee-table photo books, yet so much more color photography than simple guide books.

Each book includes:
- Colorful maps
- Valuable descriptions and charts of features such as volcanoes and glaciers
- Up-to-date understanding of environmental problems where man and nature are in conflict
- References for additional reading, agencies and offices to contact for more information
- Special sections portraying people in their homes, at work, in the countryside

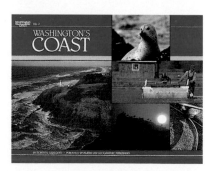

for more information write:
**American Geographic Publishing
P.O. Box 5630
Helena, Montana 59604**